IN SEARCH OF AMERICAN FOREIGN POLICY

IN SEARCH OF AMERICAN FOREIGN POLICY

THE HUMANE USE OF POWER

★ Lincoln P. Bloomfield ★

New York   Oxford University Press
London   1974   Toronto

ST. PHILIPS COLLEGE LIBRARY

Copyright © 1974 by Oxford University Press, Inc.
Library of Congress Catalogue Card Number: 73-90342
Printed in the United States of America

Some of the material in Part V is adapted from "Foreign Policy for the Disillusioned Liberal," which appeared in *Foreign Policy* No. 9, Winter 1972–73, and from "Resurrecting the United Nations," Op-Ed page, *New York Times*, July 21, 1971.

To the late
M. F. M.
who made it possible

CONTENTS

SYMPTOMS

1. Why Another Book on U.S. Foreign Policy?   3

   How To Be Schizophrenic Without Actually
   Going Mad   3
   The Perils of a Split-Level Establishmentarian   10

2. A House Divided   16

   What Do the American People Believe?   16
   New Left and Old Right   28

DIAGNOSIS

3. The Crumbling Consensus   49

   The Establishment   49
   Premises and Preconceptions   57
   Cold War Hang-ups   64

4. Where Did We Go Wrong?   75

   The American Style   75
   The Military Bias   89

And Then the Lying	99
Perils of Power	112

PRESCRIPTION

5 The Light at the End of the Tunnel	129
The Boundaries of Change	129
The Premises That Should Underlie Policy	136
Getting from Here to There	170

We are motivated, not by hatred, but by disappointment over and love for the unfulfilled potential of this nation.

> Preamble to Estes Park Report of
> White House Conference on Youth, April 1971

But in what way can one's highest loyalty be given to one's country? Surely only in one way, and that is when one wishes with all one's heart and tries with all one's powers, to make it a better country, to make it more just and more tolerant and more merciful, and if it is powerful, more wise in the use of its powers.

> Alan Paton
> at Harvard Commencement, June 17, 1971

SYMPTOMS

WHY ANOTHER BOOK ON U. S. FOREIGN POLICY?

How To Be Schizophrenic Without Actually Going Mad

It was almost time for the meeting to end when I realized that neither the Secretary of State nor the Secretary of Defense had uttered a word. Perhaps they were inhibited by the sheer size of the group; after all, Dean Rusk was said to have refused to voice his opinions to the President in any group larger than two. But why were Messrs. Rogers and Laird so reticent? Certainly, I wasn't the President.

Others didn't hold back. Under Secretary of State Elliot Richardson fell in with the spirit of the occasion. Because he was that kind of guy—and perhaps also because he was a Harvard classmate and feeling sorry for me—he plunged right in, answering my probing of U.S. foreign policy, and throwing out some questions of his own. A couple of members of the Joint Chiefs of Staff also joined the debate, although their chairman, General Earle Wheeler, saved his own words until at the end I asked him, perhaps too frivolously, to pronounce the benediction.

But mainly the ball was carried by the deputies—Assistant Secretaries of State, two-star generals and admirals, civilian agency heads, and such. After all, they were the ones who had played in the "game" over the past three weeks. Nevertheless, as chairman I became so uncomfortable with the protracted silence of the two senior Secretaries that just before the session ended I asked if they wished to add anything. The Secretary of Defense (then in office four months) replied that, as everyone knew, he always deferred to the Secretary of State on foreign policy questions. It was an open secret in Washington even by late spring of 1969 that the State Department still had not overcome the Pentagon's chronic tendency to seem to initiate foreign policy, often with a President's encouragement or at the least his indifference to Cabinet protocol. So what was meant as a pleasantry came out as heavy irony, and everyone around the table either giggled nervously or froze.

It seems incredible to me now that a meeting in Washington consisting of virtually the entire top political-military command of the United States, and including just about all the statutory senior members of the National Security Council and their deputies, should have been chaired by a professor of Political Science from the Massachusetts Institute of Technology (or, I suppose I should add, a former professor of Government from Harvard). Or for that matter by anyone but the President of the United States. Yet I was expected to chair the meeting, and I did so—after some nervous hilarity at the Pentagon's river entrance when I decided that I had to get some air and then pretended to flee just before all those long black limousines began arriving. Actually, the thought of panicky flight did cross my mind.

For my purposes here it does not really matter what the planning exercise at the Pentagon was about. I can record that it was a political-military "game" called SIGMA-I and that it took place under the auspices of the Joint Chiefs of Staff, and involved, as can be seen, the top ranks of the U.S. Government. Presumably because I knew something about both political gaming and U.S. foreign policy and could still pass a security check, I was invited

WHY ANOTHER BOOK ON FOREIGN POLICY? 5

to direct it. SIGMA-I wrestled with alternative U.S. prospects and policies in one big part of the world, and I am not allowed to say any more about it. In fact, the cast of characters is not public information either, although I suspect that the taxpayers would be glad to know that their top leaders do some long-range planning. (The Nixon Administration was new then; unfortunately, I doubt whether the top people ever went again.)

The point of the story is that, unlike the real President who went on to chair similar meetings, hold summit conferences, and run the country, when SIGMA-I ended I whistled at taxis, stood in line for the shuttle to New York, fought rush-hour traffic in Boston, and twenty-four hours later was up to my armpits in radical students and other assorted intellectuals, housewives, and suburban tradesmen—many of whom were being alienated from U.S. foreign policy not just in detail but root and branch.

Six months later I directed another high-level U.S. "game," this time in the operetta-like town of Garmisch nestled in the lee of Adolf Hitler's one-time eyrie in the Bavarian Alps. In mid-November only the first dusting of snow had fallen on the Zügspitze high above Garmisch, and in any case there was no time to envy the early skiers who clambered aboard the cog railway for the exhilarating ride up the mountain.

The players in this game—EPSILON-I—were American ambassadors and four-star generals and admirals who were stationed in Europe. It was a particularly good game, for technical reasons which have to do with all-senior games *versus* the Washington "split-level" variety, not to mention its healthy distance from the eye of the policy storm in Washington. This time, when we sat around the table at the end trying to discover what we had learned, I was delighted to see what deep roots we had exposed and shaken up. Never mind that some of the players were aghast at our undermining of some of their favorite official preconceptions about alternative probabilities in a crucial corner of Europe.

As the game director who presided over the exercise, I had a personal taste of the Hitlerian ambience that lingered in the town. Here they gave me my own aide, suite, black car and white driver, and for five days I once again exercised mock power in the role of a sympathetic though critical insider in the American foreign policy machine. Of course some academics believe that this sort of thing, by "co-opting" you to the System, corrupts you the way prostitution corrupts a woman. Corruption in oneself is hard to judge; but I must say I enjoyed the "power" in this and other "games" to force high officials to confront the dilemmas and home truths my placard-waving friends were bothered by.

At the end of EPSILON-I, after being seen off by assorted brass in Munich, I flew directly back to Boston. I was met at Logan Airport with an urgent message about an impending riot at the M.I.T. Center for International Studies, where I directed the Arms Control Project. Instead of going home to sleep off an uncommonly demanding week plus jet fatigue, I went straight to an emergency meeting of M.I.T. faculty at our Center. The next night I sat up to the small hours with our Political Science students, trying to help them—and myself—to get some perspective on their contemporaries' planned march on our Center with the avowed aim of "smashing" us. The young people most troubled were those caught between feelings of sympathy with many of the radicals' ideas about Vietnam, intervention, government, and "imperialism," and of distaste for facing those problems by blasting buildings, rioting, or abusing individual faculty members.

In the twelve years since I had left the State Department to become an M.I.T. professor and researcher, I never got closer to my students than in those turbulent few days. It was as though all accumulated tensions finally fused and for a while were the dominant reality. Titular authority was meaningless unless it could prove its intrinsic legitimacy. Helping the U.S. Government as a consultant or adviser or contract researcher was prima facie proof of complicity in evil unless proven to the contrary. In this atmosphere, at all age-levels, passion seemed in danger of replacing rea-

WHY ANOTHER BOOK ON FOREIGN POLICY? 7

son. Those who kept their cool—but stayed with it and tried to do something constructive—became heroic figures.

Two of our politically most alienated younger people had spent half the night sewing an enormous banner from old sheets, rather in the manner of Betsy Ross. The banner spelled out the words that the large majority of us had been able to agree on after all the talk had been spent. The emblazoned message proclaimed that we favored open discussion of all issues, wanted a ceasefire in Vietnam, supported the right of everyone in a university to dissent and express opinions however controversial, and considered violence an unacceptable means of persuasion.

The climax came in mid-morning at the east end of the M.I.T. campus, at the Hermann Building housing our Center. It was raining lightly that morning. About a hundred of us—Political Science faculty, Center researchers, students, secretaries, and staff—stood under the banner huddled in our raincoats on the damp grass outside the building. We all wore blue armbands symbolizing our solidarity (no one could explain the significance of the color). Not all the Political Science faculty or Center senior staff were there. A few were so outraged by the very idea of militant student protest that they rejected any notion of discussion, compromise, or common ground as well.

Nor were all the students there. Some, even in 1969, were still in the tradition of M.I.T. "tools"—short-haired, politically conservative, and that day studying somewhere else because the M.I.T. administration had sealed off our building. Some other students—and faculty—were in the mass we could see first as a tiny black and shapeless spot at the other end of Ames Street, gradually advancing until everyone could make out the leather jackets and army boots and placards, and hear the screaming denunciation by the youthful Madame de Farge atop a sound truck, and feel the thrill and the animal fear of impending collision between two antagonistic bodies of human beings.

In the end our little knot of supporters of change, non-violence, and rational discourse was virtually ignored. Above us on the broad plaza leading into the building were deployed M.I.T.'s battalions of deans, reinforced campus police, plain-clothes detectives, walkie-talkies, bullhorns, photographers, newsmen, TV cameras, and all the rest of the ritual counterinsurgency apparatus of the urban American university of the late 1960s. Predictably, the mob's leaders headed for the cameras as to a magnet.

And so the marchers got their kicks from facing, not the ambiguous liberals, but the genuine pigs. Some did deign to face us, grinning sheepishly through their hostility. We looked in vain for the bicycle chains the Weathermen were going to carry to "trash" our place of work and study, and perhaps us as well.

Well, they didn't "smash" C.I.S. as they had promised to do. In fact, I think now that some of the potential for violence had been defused a month before when the first anti-C.I.S. "mill-in" took place. Then, several hundred marchers including students, faculty, assorted deans, curious onlookers, plain-clothes men, photographers, newsmen, and all the rest had actually invaded our Center.

For almost an entire day we stopped work. Some went home. But some of us stayed to protect our research papers, and so fell into what turned out to be a useful if unorthodox opportunity for serious debate and attempted explanation of exactly what we "warmongers" actually did, and why most of it was work that anyone preferring peace to war, development to poverty, and arms control to arms races should support rather than try to smash. In truth some of the Center's research *had* concerned counterinsurgency and means to support official Vietnam policy. I myself had published a letter in the *New York Times* in 1965 supporting the policy of preventing a takeover by force in South Vietnam no less than in those other divided countries, Korea and Germany. By 1967, however, I was among the drafters of the so-called "Bermuda Declaration," in which a group of American centrists urged on President Johnson cessation of bombing and a coalition government in Vietnam.

WHY ANOTHER BOOK ON FOREIGN POLICY?

I frankly do not want to spend many more such hours facing a hostile, glandular crowd packed into a hallway on the fourth floor of a disaster-prone building that featured dangerous cul-de-sacs, misplaced exits, and sealed windows, and pushing Vietcong flags away from my face as I tried to debate, explain, and expostulate. Still, I think it was time well spent. Many of the students who came in ignorance, anger, or curiosity found out that what the Students for a Democratic Society (SDS) and the Weathermen and other militant groups had been feeding them about us was at best distorted propaganda, at worst downright lies.

But I must also record my own personal rediscovery of the extent to which the evident lack of human concern in current U.S. foreign behavior, from instrument bombing in Vietnam to exploitive overseas investments, so tortured a number of our bright young people that they were willing to put their bodies on the line against it. These young people (and many older and equally concerned people) were often appallingly ignorant of historic fact, and usually substituted sentimentality for reason in their thinking. Yet much of what I have to say in this book is devoted to the need they correctly felt to restore human concern to America's world role.

I am by no means so tolerant of faculty members who led students in disruptive assaults on intellectual activities in their own university. On this occasion the debate evidently became so well-behaved and so reasonable that an M.I.T. colleague who was a ringleader of the "mill-in" rounded up some of his hard-line cohorts to re-enter the hall and shout me down with ritual leftist obscenities and battle cries. My university, in a fit of determined fair-mindedness, shortly thereafter rewarded the same intellectual arsonist with promotion to full professor on the ground that his professional qualifications were unchallengeable. I am reminded that yet another M.I.T. colleague and hero of the New Left intellectuals during that period asserted in my presence that he would not hesitate to blow up the laboratory of a colleague whose work he disapproved of. So much for "Make love not war."

The Perils of a Split-Level Establishmentarian

It may be thought that I am being excessively personal about all this—hardly the done thing in foreign policy analysis (as distinguished from memoir writing, for which I have no credentials). Yet perhaps after reading the foregoing confessions you can see why I feel like a man caught in the middle, one foot planted in each of two bitterly divided camps, catching flak from both sides of the argument, chronically marching to two different drums. Having spent half my working life in government and the other half so far as a teacher, I was no stranger to this vivid sense of contrast, of living in two worlds, of doing the split aboard two horses both labeled "U.S. foreign policy" but each going in a different direction. But in the late 1960s and early 1970s the feeling of schizophrenia became overwhelming.

Part of this is "role-playing"—and both bureaucrats and academics do it. Cambridge intellectuals McGeorge Bundy, Walt Rostow, and Henry Kissinger became super-bureaucrats and politicians when they served as Presidential right arms. In reverse, the ex-bureaucrat who moves to a university soon begins to feel his critical juices flowing. He may even become a dues-paying, card-carrying intellectual fascinated with theories, models, and ideas, and for that reason deemed irrelevant and even dangerous by his former associates.

A special trap awaits one who tries to do both simultaneously, i.e., when he professes to be a foreign policy scholar, but directs his efforts not only to theory building and teaching but to action as well, and tries to be effective by working with rather than against those inside the policy machine. However good his contacts, he never knows whether anything he writes or says or advises is affecting things where they really matter—though of course some insiders have the same problem. Meanwhile, his rear and flanks are extraordinarily vulnerable. And unless he stays in

WHY ANOTHER BOOK ON FOREIGN POLICY?

such exotic compounds as Cambridge, Massachusetts, the assaults will likely come from both extremes, often for the same sin (such as, e.g., actively supporting the United Nations).

I myself have been marched on and reviled by the radical left as a bloody fascist imperialist out to smash popular revolutions; and hanging in my basement at home is an expensively turned-out SDS poster with a flattering photograph of me, along with my colleagues William Griffith, Lucian Pye, and Everett Hagen, under the blazing words "WANTED FOR SERVING U.S. IMPERIALISM." During those same 1960s I was also denounced as a pinko, soft on Communism, and hot on world government. I was once picketed by the John Birch Society and the American Nazi Party (in Cincinnati) for speaking on United Nations Day. And, if you had put a dime in any pay-phone in the environs of Indianapolis in August 1971, you would have heard a recorded message sponsored by a patriotic group labeled LET FREEDOM RING, accusing me of being a "termite" who burrows into the soft, unsuspecting fabric of American life with a plot to impose a Communistic U.N. dictatorship (President Nixon was implicated also in this plot).

There is more. I have been grilled for hours on end by State Department security officers because I worked in a bureau in the Deparment that once was headed by Alger Hiss, my first boss in the Department. And I was anathematized by one John A. Stormer in his best-selling lunatic-fringe book *None Dare Call It Treason* (Florissant, Mo.: Liberty Bell Press, 1964) for fostering supranationalism as well as for belonging to the ("Communistic") Council on Foreign Relations. Some among my short-haired—and highly intelligent—audience at the National War College in Washington (where I lecture every year) believe that my long-haired students are doubtless reds, and that I am probably tainted too. But of course some of my students and colleagues consider me a tool of the hated military-industrial complex whenever I don a tuxedo and go to the absurdly stuffy (but often instructive) dinner meetings at the Park Avenue mansion of that same Council on Foreign Relations.

I do in fact favor the United Nations, arms control, and—if I thought it were possible, which I don't short of a catastrophic war —disarmament and limited world government as well. And I consult for the State Department and other government agencies, and I have run planning games for the U.S. Government (*and* for the International Peace Academy *and* the Carnegie Endowment for International Peace *and* the Institute of the United States of America of the Soviet Academy of Sciences). More, I have developed a computer system called CASCON to help avert international violence, and it could be used to aid in suppressing insurgencies although it is not intended to; and I have given it to the United Nations as well as to the U.S. Government (which paid for it), and Soviet officials have told me that it is the most useful system of its kind they have seen, as have some Third World diplomats who would like their nations to be left alone by their neighbors and local terrorists.

And, just to get it all on the table, I *do* admire the quality of mind and character of many American bureaucrats every bit as much as I share many of the critiques of my fellow academicians. I can respect both, even when I disagree with them—*except* when the bureaucrat forgets his common humanity, which has happened quite a lot in recent years; and when the academic forgets his common sense, which also has happened quite a lot recently. I have not only marched but also danced to both drums, and know the musical scores by heart. But I cannot bring myself wholly to accept either, or wholly to condemn either.

It seems reasonable, in the face of all this, to ask whether I am merely insensitive and opportunistic, or genuinely mad. But after all, isn't such ambivalence a reflection of the innermost national problem about foreign policy? Doesn't it symbolize the split in the community that still cares about our world role, a community torn between the mind that sees the realities and the heart that

WHY ANOTHER BOOK ON FOREIGN POLICY?

cries out for reform? Even in the midst of governmental turmoil, with attention increasingly distracted by scandal or beguiled by summitry, is there not still the obligation somehow to deal with the continuing polarities in American opinion on foreign policy, somehow to untangle the contradictions in policy itself?

What follows is about American foreign policy because I believe that certain changes in our conception of American foreign policy can go far toward restoring both our internal morale and our world reputation. I should also like to be proud again of the American role and contribution in the world. On this exploration my preferred companions are those who are too well informed to believe that everything is really OK, too stable to feel that it is all hopeless, too intelligent to believe in the "quick fix," and too modest to be certain that they have all the answers. These are the people who try to keep informed, care what is happening, feel that despite spectaculars in superpower relations the United States seems to have lost its way elsewhere, love their country, do not really trust their leaders, and want to know what can be done about it.

From about December 1941 until the early 1960s there was a wide-ranging consensus on U.S. foreign policy that embraced all Presidents, most bureaucrats, most members of the Congress, many journalists and editorial writers, some academics, and most voters. In broad terms it was internationalist, financially generous, global-thinking, U.N.-supportive and institution-building, deterrence-minded, at least verbally democracy-preferring, anti-Communist, and above all, committed to oppose isolationism. The so-called "Establishment" gave it both doctrine and direction; yet in a sense, except for the far left and 'way-out right, it was all of America—at least for a while.

If we need a shorthand label for it, my unenthusiastic choice is the "liberal approach" to foreign policy—unenthusiastic because "liberal," self-defined as "progressive" and humane, usually prefers to focus on domestic problem-solving. Indeed, a globally interventionist foreign policy is a kind of corruption of liberalism. For the same reason, this definition doesn't precisely correspond to classic self-defined liberalism such as that of John Stuart Mill and Jeremy Bentham, the New York Liberal Party, the British Liberal Association, or all Americans who have considered themselves liberals with a small "l." Now "liberal" has become a dirty word to the alienated left, just as it always was in the eyes of the political right. Nevertheless, because it encapsulates a rather well-defined policy strategy that Americans first accepted and then increasingly came to question, "liberal" is used here to sum up the foreign policy consensus initiated with Franklin D. Roosevelt, made bipartisan by the conversion of former isolationist Republican Senator Arthur H. Vandenberg, and ended with the war in Indochina.

What I am calling here the liberal approach to U.S. foreign policy flourished through the Truman, Eisenhower, Kennedy, and Johnson administrations, and in many ways it persisted into the Nixon Administration. By the mid-1950s it had begun to be questioned in some particulars; by the mid-1960s it was being challenged in more basic detail; and by the mid-1970s it stood as a ghost of its former self. No one seemed to know whether it simply needed a nourishing meal and a few words of encouragement, along with minor tinkering with programs; or whether it was in fact a terminal case, moving on inertia alone, and bereft of its inner force and meaning for the nation.

The fact that *American* policy is here discussed is not to imply that no other nation deserves criticism. No nation in the world is blameless. And the corollary of Murphy's Law—so widespread in recent years—is in the main unjustified. (For the uninitiated, Murphy's Law says: "If something can go wrong, it will"; the corollary added: "And it's the United States' fault.")

What we need now is a new synthesis out of the mix of old-established wisdom (so much of which turned out to be unwise) and the pressures for change (so many of which seem naïve or unrealistic). Since those in charge of policy do not seem to have come up with it, my own effort here is to seek out that light at the end of the policy tunnel, in the conviction that America's world role is, for better or worse, likely to be a determining factor in the future as in the past.

★ 2 ★

A HOUSE DIVIDED

What Do the American People Believe?

Historically, relatively few Americans ever focused in serious detail on the U.S. world role. As the nation, beset by political scandals, inflation, and other domestic concerns, turned inward, there were nevertheless signs of deep-seated changes in attitudes, especially among the young.

The evidence of the early 1970s showed a widespread unhappiness with certain aspects of the U.S. world role, along with pervasive mistrust of government, which Watergate massively accentuated. Even so, it was staggering to learn that in January 1971, according to a Gallup Poll, "as many as four college students in every 10 think change in America during the next 25 years is more likely to occur through a revolution than through peaceful means" (*New York Times*, January 20, 1971). Forty-four per cent of all the students Gallup interviewed felt that violence is sometimes justified to bring about change in American society. Two years later, after the Vietnam War had officially ended, another Gallup Poll found three out of ten college-trained Americans between 18 and 29 wanting to leave the United States and settle elsewhere.

A HOUSE DIVIDED

Those figures were more than enough to confirm the worst fears of any middle-class suburbanite. The locker-room Cassandras had been telling us that all too many modern youth were subversive, unpatriotic, ungrateful, destructive, and intolerant of the slow processes of democracy. But, in that same 1971 poll, eight in ten of the *same student group* said that they took pride in being Americans, with a large majority in each section of the country expressing such patriotic feelings.

How reconcile these conflicting statistics? Were these young people just exploiting the panic we Establishmentarians got into at the thought of civil violence? (*Why*, my young friends kept asking during the riotous years, don't you get as uptight about injustice?) At all events, a whopping eight out of ten in the 1971 survey believed that the American political system does not respond quickly enough to meet the needs of the people.

In October of that same year, *Newsweek* analyzed a set of polls under the heading "Profile of the New Voter." What became overwhelmingly clear from the results was that the young people held sharply defined—and unorthodox—notions of what is important and what is not—in other words, the priorities. Overwhelmingly they wanted more tax money spent on cleaning up the environment, helping the unemployed, Medicare, housing for the poor, and (believe it or not) coping with crime. They wanted far less spent on military defense and foreign economic aid. Sixty-eight per cent wanted less spent on space exploration, 64 per cent wanted less spent on foreign military aid.

That same year a poll of 57,000 high-school and junior high-school students showed much the same sense of priorities. Air pollution and water pollution were rated the nation's top problems, followed by the Vietnam War, drug abuse, and race relations, with Communism ranked last in eight possible categories of priority (*New York Times*, January 10, 1971). This response could well be called isolationism; in fact, that is just what it was. Yet curiously it failed to correlate with the neo-isolationism of the "radical liberal" American left. These high-school people turned out to be not predominantly leftist, but clustered at the center, much like their elders: 20 per cent very conservative, 45 per cent middle of the road, 28 per cent "liberal radical left."

Much of this dropping out from world concerns was a two-sided switch. Vietnam's message to them was that U.S. foreign policy was wrong, not just in detail, but at root; and at the same time youthful attention became riveted on domestic problems. Thus, for example, undergraduate enrollment in international relations courses dropped precipitously at M.I.T. with each new year of the 1970s, while shooting up successively in urban problems, ecology, and other "social action" subjects. The outside world may still have been there; but students (like people) are notoriously single-minded.

The research of a perceptive young Harvard professor named Graham Allison confirmed this switch: "The current preoccupations of our youth [unlike their preoccupations of the 1940s, 1950s, or early 1960s] are predominantly, pervasively, and indeed almost entirely *not* issues of foreign policy. Problems of foreign affairs (with the exception of Vietnam) are not what young Americans think about, care about, or hope to spend their public lives doing something about." He went on to say something even more relevant to the present inquiry:

> To the extent that foreign policy is currently important to young Americans, their posture stresses a generalized desire to "cool" foreign affairs. They want Vietnam over, defense budgets down, international entanglements cut. Their reading of the consequences of past foreign policies reinforces their argument for new domestic priorities. Hence *they challenge the guidelines that have governed American foreign policy in the postwar era* and they insist that the empire which emerged as a consequence of those guidelines be drastically shrunk. ("Cool It: The Foreign Policy of Young America," *Foreign Policy*, Winter 1970-71, p. 148; italics are mine)

Allison seems to have concentrated on a select group of college-educated youth, and we might conclude, as in another context Spiro Agnew and his followers seemed to, that these were "effete intellectual snobs" of the Eastern Seaboard Left whose views were not only contemptible but trivial alongside those of the "real" young American. In this view the "real" American boy may not go to college but does honest work. If he does go to college he sensibly subscribes to the policies and the worldviews of the Establishment. Moreover, he is short-haired, neatly dressed, and respectful to his elders.

The April 1971 White House Conference on Youth assembled at Estes Park, Colorado, as many people as possible who looked like that. College students comprised only 20 per cent of the fifteen hundred delegates. High-school students constituted 40 per cent, working young people about 35 per cent, and military 5 per cent. The first surprise came with the reports of representative delegates who had been asked to do research on the problems in advance of the conference.

One such study group concluded that, in their Report's words, those who shape U.S. foreign policy have been frozen in a "reflexive anti-communism," leading to the "ugly" embroilment in Vietnam, a "distorted sense of the national interest," and division and ferment at home. That group urged the United States to "admit mistakes openly instead of making vain attempts to rectify error in judgments under the guise of saving the country from defeat." It went on to say that the President must adopt a policy of "complete consultation" with the Senate about any military commitments abroad. Another study group suggested that the United Nations police the world to control what they termed any "environmentally damaging actions" committed by any member that would be harmful to all (*New York Times*, April 11, 1971).

When the Conference ended on April 21, 1971, literally hundreds of recommendations had been made by the various task forces, including one call for a drastic scaling down of the defense budget to $50 billion. A number of outside observers were particularly struck by the preamble to the final report, which apparently received a one-minute standing ovation after it had been read to the delegates. Charging that the "high ideals upon which this country was founded have never been a reality for all peoples from the beginning to the present day," it listed in detail the shortcomings that the Conference had identified as having undermined American ideals.

The statement was immediately denounced by Senator Wm. E. Brock of Tennessee as "masochistic, negative, and non-productive." His reaction, in the context, recalled Voltaire's Dr. Pangloss, who instructed his pupil Candide that "private misfortunes contribute to the general good, so that the more private misfortunes there are, the more we find that all is well."

The Estes Park conferees, like all young people, exaggerated the problems that bothered them, demanded unrealistic solutions, and neglected to catalog the things that are right about American society. Even so, I cannot think of any of us "realistic" Establishmentarians who have quite matched the spirit of the final sentence of the Estes Park report. "We are motivated," it read, "not by hatred, but by disappointment over and love for the unfulfilled potential of this nation."

Coincidentally, during the same month of April 1971, another Establishment-run conference of young people took place. It was also in Colorado, at the Air Force Academy nestled under the Rockies near Colorado Springs, where sudden snow squalls in April blot out spring for one minute and vanish in the next. This particular meeting, an intercollegiate discussion of current Caribbean problems, was the thirteenth such annual conference sponsored by the Academy. The students attending those conferences are both bright and representative of a broad sector of America. The interesting thing about the 1971 conference was that most of the participating cadets, as well as the visiting West Point cadets and Naval Academy midshipmen, pushed hard for what became known at the conference as the "liberal position." The final report virtually without dissent recommended that the United States foreswear military intervention in the Caribbean and seek to resume full relations with Cuba (*New York Times*, April 19, 1971).

Again, a detailed inquiry into the state of youthful American opinion was reported in the work *Youth and the Establishment*, sponsored by that impeccably Establishmentarian leader and spokesman, John D. Rockefeller III (New York: J. D. Rockefeller Fund, 1971). It pinpointed the enormous effect that one traumatic year—1969 to 1970—had not only on young American intellectuals (the "forerunners") whom one could expect to be most disaffected and critical, but also on the career-minded. Queried about "Objectives Worth Fighting For," in 1969 55 per cent of the "career minded" responded that "containing the Communists" was worth fighting for. But a year later the number was down to 41 per cent.

Even while President Nixon was issuing periodic injunctions to Americans to guard their position as "Number One in the world," only 25 per cent of the entire group believed in 1969 that "Maintaining Our Position of Power in the World" was worth fighting for; and by 1970 the percentage had dropped to a startling 17 per cent (with 59 per cent of the "forerunner" group positively repudiating the objectives). Roughly the same figures applied to "Fighting for Our Honor," with 61 per cent of the "forerunners" saying it is not worth fighting for.

It was tempting to compare this with the notorious 1933 resolution by the Oxford Union, "Resolved: that this House will in no circumstance fight for King and Country." When the chips were down several years later, that posturing was quite forgotten. Yet I did wonder just what kind of challenge to the U.S. power position or national "honor" is likely to change the minds of these young leadership types. I suspend judgment. But from what I know of the youth involved, their attitude cannot be taken as a suggestion that the United States act dishonorably, or that honor *per se* is a worthless value. It was that their definition of "honor" was at wide variance with Mr. Nixon's.

Some other Rockefeller findings are also interesting. In 1969 only 16 per cent of the whole group felt that "The War in Vietnam Is Pure Imperialism," but a year later the figure had jumped to 41 per cent (50 per cent of the "forerunners"). This trend doubtless correlated with the feeling of almost half the group in 1970 that U.S. foreign policy is based on narrow economic and power interests. (Here our young friends were on shakier ground, mainly because they don't understand what pure imperialism is, which in turn is a result of their often monumental ignorance of both history and comparative politics. Their views would make more sense if they understood that the trouble with recent American foreign policy is that it has been *impure* imperialism. It has given this nation few of the classic economic advantages of imperialism such as guaranteed markets, non-competitive cheap labor, and assured natural resources on preferential terms. Or demographic advantages of colonies for surplus population export. Or security advantages such as reliable military and naval bases. But it has given the nation most of the disadvantages of projecting "power interests" in situations that turn out to be not very amenable to U.S. military power.)

The extent to which American young people expressed willingness to drop out from the world scene was driven home graphically in the Rockefeller report. Forty-eight per cent of the whole sample (58 per cent of the "forerunners") were willing to make a personal commitment (such as donating a year or two of service) to fighting poverty. But only 8 per cent would make such personal commitment to controlling armaments, 9 per cent to bringing peace to the Middle East, and 7 per cent to helping the Third World we hear so much about from them. These figures correlate accurately with the percentage of the over-all group that wanted any kind of significant relation with members of the Executive Branch of the Federal Government: a pathetic 5 per cent. I do not know a single more depressing fact about the current college generation, although I admit being prejudiced.

Just after graduating from Harvard in 1941 I was recruited by a dynamic bureaucrat named Milo Perkins, who believed in bringing young "interns" into his U.S. Surplus Marketing Administration. Mr. Perkins really believed in Youth Power, and within six months I was in charge of the Federal Food Stamp Plan and School Lunch Program for the state of Oregon. For me the ideal of government/public/community service was intoxicating. Including service in the Navy during World War II it lasted sixteen years—until my experience in John Foster Dulles' State Department, complete with police surveillance and silly, hypocritical policy actions, persuaded me to abandon it as a full-time career. (Sixteen years later White House aide Gordon Strachan tearfully told the Senate Select Committee on Watergate that his advice to young people was to "stay away.")

Who is going to man the Government and help make this a better country? Who is going to serve? Who is going to bring to U.S. foreign policy the necessary changed attitudes and approaches? It may be that the single most expensive societal cost ascribable to Indochina, including the governmental deception that went along with it, took the form of massive abstention by alarming numbers of bright and qualified young Americans from recruitment to U.S. foreign policy agencies and programs.

How different are the views of older Americans? Most of the polls report that on the big issues the young do not see things all that differently from at least some of their elders. A national poll in late 1972 by Cambridge Survey Research reported 70 per cent as agreeing that "America needs drastic change to get going again." Very much like the young, 85 per cent of the leading citizens surveyed in thirty-four American cities in 1971 by the Council on Foreign Relations favored efforts to establish a *modus vivendi*

with the U.S.S.R.; unlike the young, however, they would make it contingent upon specifics. Another 41 per cent felt that the United States, while maintaining its nuclear deterrent and conventional military power, ought to try through the SALT talks and otherwise to "stabilize the military balance"—a formulation not heard often from younger people. Another 44 per cent felt that while maintaining nuclear deterrence the United States should reduce its conventional power. Going farther, this group advocated that the United States "review its worldwide commitments to decrease chances of the involvement of U.S. forces in local conflicts."

In the same survey only 3.5 per cent felt the United States should "do its utmost to prevent the expansion of Soviet power, relying primarily on military strength." Perhaps most surprising of all, only 13 per cent saw the Soviet Union as still a military threat to the United States and its allies, or as a revolutionary power bent on expansion (more about this later). One of the most striking surveys focused on 456 of the most affluent, most powerful, most influential people in the country. When taken in August 1972 by Columbia University's Bureau of Applied Social Research, this poll found two-thirds agreeing that the U.S. has sometimes contributed to the Cold War by overreacting to Soviet moves or military developments—an erosion of older beliefs.

While all this reflected substantial changes in conventional attitudes, the polls uncovered little outright isolationist sentiment, and many Americans even agreed with President Nixon that the United States should strive to be "Number One"—67 per cent, according to a *Wall Street Journal* survey conducted by Trendex in November 1971. But more than 30 per cent responded that, as a general concept, the idea of being Number One simply wasn't important to them. The reasons given are interesting in contrast to the New Left's critique. A majority of those who believed that America should be first in everything responded that they felt that way for reasons of morale, prestige, or patriotism. A trivial

5.6 per cent cited possible economic benefits, and only 8.9 per cent cited reasons having to do with maintaining peace (see *Wall Street Journal*, November 16, 1971). So much for both Economic Man and the United States as World Gendarme, at least among these Americans.

It is of course common knowledge that the same question asked in different ways can elicit contradictory answers. Yet there is strong evidence of deep-seated opposition to American military intervention in all manner of situations around the world—situations that my M.I.T. associate Amelia Leiss and I some years ago christened "local conflicts" (a label that seems to have stuck). The Administration negotiated admirable if unenforceable agreements with Moscow in 1972 and 1973, offering the hope that both would abstain from such interventionism. But public opinion went far beyond "local conflicts" into the realm often called "vital interests." A poll conducted by *Time* magazine in May 1969 posed hypothetical questions about invasion of friendly countries by Communist military forces. If Thailand, for example, were invaded by outside Communist military forces, only 25 per cent of those polled favored sending U.S. troops to her support; if Italy, 27 per cent; if West Berlin, 26 per cent. And if Israel were in danger of being overrun by Soviet-aided Arabs, only 9 per cent of those answering would favor sending American troops to her help. I found Israeli officials still stunned by this poll in 1972, and many Americans ambiguous about it when the fighting broke out again in October 1973.

With the U.S. out of Vietnam much of the virulence seemed to drain out of dissent about foreign policy. The Administration was properly credited for improving U.S. relations with Russia and China. But the evidence continued to mount that the country was turning inward. A comprehensive survey on the "State of the Nation" in 1973 found a remarkable 87 per cent of Americans in the poll agreeing that the United States, while continuing to be a major world influence, should cut down some of its responsibilities abroad (Potomac Associates, 1973); and a June 1973 Gallup Poll reported 55 per cent believing that the United States should "stop getting involved in other countries' affairs." A more pointed opinion was expressed by 84 per cent of America's leading business executives, who "disagreed completely" with the notion of deep U.S. military involvement in the Third World" (Cetron and Overly in *Technology Review*, March/April 1973).

★ ★ ★ ★

During his incumbency at City Hall Mayor John Lindsay of New York probably saw more live city-dwellers than anyone in Washington *or* Cambridge, Massachusetts. Here are some words Mr. Lindsay wrote about the generation spawned by Vietnam a year before Watergate broke into the public consciousness. His point was that this generation has lost faith in *all* government, including the admittedly impossible one he tried to run.

> . . . it is a generation united by disillusion and not only by age, which cannot believe that *any* government is capable of *any* act motivated by genuine desire to improve the lot of the people. The reader who feels this is overdrawn is invited to walk, as I have, through the neighborhoods of our great cities. He will find that this disillusion pervades all ages, income classes, philosophies and occupations. Conspiracy theories abound and gain widespread credence no matter how ludicrous or implausible. Wholesomeness and trustworthiness are defined in terms of distance from governmental influence. . . . What remains to be seen is whether credible and committed leadership can restore the self-respect of a people so sorely diminished in their own eyes. ("For a New Policy Balance," *Foreign Affairs*, October 1971, p. 6)

President Nixon in his State of the Union address in January 1972 announced that the mood was now changing. Comparing it with that of the late 1960s, he stated that "Then we were a shaken and uncertain people, but now we are recovering our confidence." Perhaps unconsciously picking up a favorite Kennedy

A HOUSE DIVIDED

quote from Yeats (plus some hip slang), he added, "The 'center' of American life has held and once again we are getting ourselves together."

He could be right, even with Watergate (or perhaps because of it). Public opinion polls can be misleading, and what Canning called "the fatal artillery of public excitation" is notoriously fickle. I myself hold to Abraham Lincoln's belief in the rightness of popular sentiment over time, although sobered as I am by Walter Lippmann's warnings about the "malady of democratic states." As that wise man wrote,

> The unhappy truth is that the prevailing public opinion has been destructively wrong at the critical junctures. The people have imposed a veto upon the judgments of informed and responsible officials. They have compelled the governments, which usually knew what would have been wiser, or was necessary, or was more expedient, to be too late with too little, or too long with too much, too pacifist in peace, and too bellicose in war, too neutralist or too appeasing, or too intransigent.

That sort of argument is pretty unacceptable to those mistrustful of government generally and alienated from the bureaucratic elite's notions of reality as chronicled, for instance, in the Pentagon Papers. Perhaps one has to take Lincoln and Lippmann together. A plausible long view is that, after the dust of both Watergate and the Indochina war finally settles (to use Dean Acheson's least successful phrase), the United States will once again be able to play an influential world role, with the domestic support of all but a few freaky holdouts in the counterculture.

And yet, what if the malaise in U.S. public opinion is not just a phase in the cycle (along the lines of the famous twenty-seven-year alternation of "extroversion" and "introversion" phases of U.S. foreign policy posited by Frank L. Klingberg (in his article "The Historical Alternation of Moods in American Foreign Policy," in *World Politics*, January 1952)? What if it coincides with a significant change in the "objective conditions" (as the Communists like to say) of the world scene? What if the mood of many Americans was not merely a momentary revulsion from the interminable Vietnam War, but rather a correct sensing—authentic to Mr. Lincoln—that some underlying assumptions governing U.S. foreign policy during the past thirty or so years were no longer really appropriate to the changing world?

The issue, then, is not the fluctuating and fickle findings of polls, which will doubtless change again when the post-Vietnam generation of young Americans graduates and votes. The issue is how we as a nation are to adapt our foreign policy both to external change *and* to a definition of national purpose that we can once again agree upon.

To analyze this vital conjunction: I think that the root of the matter is to be found in *underlying assumptions* about both the nature of the world and America's proper role in it. It is there, more than anywhere else, that a deep gulf has opened between government and outside critics, between factions within government, and between the sectors of what might be called the "foreign policy community," in which are found concerned professionals and others in and outside government. Underlying assumptions are painfully hard to discover and to debate. Most people—including most people in the foreign policy community—do not seem fully aware of the premises of their own thinking. But those premises are indisputably the most important elements of all in learning—and deciding—which way the wind is to blow.

New Left and Old Right

Americans with strong opinions about foreign policy certainly have been giving the impression of being more polarized than any time in recent memory, except when the battle lines were drawn in the late 1930s on whether to help Britain fight Hitler. It wasn't very long ago that the sides of the argument were well-defined.

A HOUSE DIVIDED

There was the Soviet-sympathetic left, the "fortress America" right, and the consensus center. Left and right are still there, and I shall come to them in a moment (and the center, in the next chapter). What has really changed is the nature of the argument.

Not very far out from the center are those lined up on one side of the foreign policy argument who want the United States to drop out and "turn inward." That they include both leftists and centrists is really not the point. The point is that here are found the urbanists as well as the objects of their concern in the slums, the people focusing on the drug culture, the rural populists, the labor union foreign-trade protectionists, and, in addition, those millions of Americans either bored to death with crusades or disgusted to the point of avoidance with the results of America's "world role."

Lined up on the other side are, crudely speaking, the holdover international relations buffs—like me, I guess—who keep saying that the outside world is still there, it is full of conflicts, nuclear weapons can still kill us all, we have to buy and sell abroad, and anyway a responsible power cannot simply curl up and go to sleep (why not, by the way?). And among the internationalists are found other passionate categories: the status quo-ers *versus* the reformers; the go-it-aloners *versus* the multilateralists; the Europe-firsters *versus* the Asia-focused; the diplomatists *versus* the functionalists; and the balancers of power *versus* the global humanists.

The fractionating of the already small "foreign affairs community" has further dissipated its national influence. But what particularly depresses me about my brethren (and perhaps about myself as well) is the predictability of our views, no less than those of the extremists. Sometimes all seem to be playing a foreordained role scripted by some celestial director. Who can count the number of academics who, after being in Washington fulltime for a few weeks, announce that people on the outside simply can't know the realities of responsibility, can't have all the facts, don't understand the pressures on a President, and so on? (The chronic version of this syndrome is, of course, found among most foreign policy professionals *inside* government.)

Equally predictable is the Pavlovian reaction of other academics in their native habitat when fed key buzz-words like "State Department," "deterrence," "balance of power," "strategy," even "diplomacy." And it is hardly worth commenting on the predictability of professional "realists" in the face of such catnip as "disarmament," "the U.N.," "social justice," "social theory," or for that matter any "theory."

The people I am thinking of are quite well informed, and often supply apt illustrations of Mark Twain's observation that "it ain't ignorance that causes all the trouble, it's that people know so dang much that ain't so." Their kind of invincible ignorance is, of course, most typical of political extremes, where all explanations end in conspiracy theory. But it is encountered also in places that leave one breathless with its implications. At the height of the recent academic dissent a well-known U.S. four-star general asserted in my presence that American student radicals were "basically pro-Soviet." In the same period, presumably well-educated undergraduate-level instructors in the social sciences asserted with equal conviction that U.S. foreign policies are governed exclusively by economic greed. Both statements are so ludicrously wrong as to be caricatures. Both the general and the dissenter had hold of scraps of the truth, but distorted them into political fantasy. Both held a firm picture inside their heads, based on their experience, reading, and prejudices, a picture that was out of register with objective reality. The general's picture was acquired in the 1930s, 1940s, and perhaps early 1950s—a time when significant numbers of U.S. radicals *did* have direct ties with Moscow, and when the world-wide Communist movement *was* indeed world-wide. If he had even noticed the Sino-Soviet split, let alone the warring factions among U.S. Marxists or Maoists, Rosa Luxemburgists, Che Guevarists, Fidelistas (*and* paid Moscow agents), he would not have sounded quite so kooky a practitioner of what Jeremy Bentham called "the art of being methodically ignorant of what everyone knows."

As for the all-out economic determinist, the picture in that head was a mishmash of actual economic fact twisted to fit 1916-vintage Leninist theories of imperialism, plus an infusion of fantastic underground newsprint (and possibly a psychic need to believe that American grownups are inherently evil). In both cases—to steal a line from that splendid script for the film *Desperate Characters*—my knowledge is no match for their ignorance. My four-star general and my social-science radical both belong to the "foreign policy community" as I have defined it here. Both are professionally engaged in it, and both have claims to be taken seriously because they operate within its key institutions. But both of them express views that stretch well out from the political center to the misty fringes of the spectrum.

To take the general first. He reflects a point of view that cannot be dismissed as wholly evil or unimportant, no matter how much one may disagree with it. The group he speaks for includes the inflexible Cold Warriors to the right who fear as traps all serious efforts toward détente with the two great Communist powers, specifically including the summit agreements reached by their hero-turned-soft, Richard Nixon. His group includes also the diplomatic tacticians whose lifetime of negotiating with the Communists has made them more than a little cynical, and who moreover do not want any amateurs mixing into their recondite business.

The general's constituency certainly includes supermilitarists whose prescriptions for "overwhelming U.S. military superiority" would condemn us to an unending arms race and possibly a nuclear war (which they still assert can be "won"). It also includes the unreconstructed interventionists who still dream imperialist dreams of the "American Century" and "Pax Americana."

What these all have in common is the conviction that the Cold War is far from over; that the Soviet Union and the People's

Republic of China remain fundamentally hostile to the West; that since the Russians understand and respect only force, U.S. military power must remain clearly superior to that of the U.S.S.R. The corollary is that the game is world-wide—dominoes all. Thus they consistently supported the war in Vietnam. At a maximum it could be "won." At a minimum South Vietnam had to be held by the "free world."

The world is thus a checkerboard (chess is too subtle), and U.S.-Communist relations are what the game theorists like to call "zero-sum": every gain is the other fellow's loss, and *vice versa*. Whereas, those of us working on arms control problems in recent years soon learned that the only effective approach was precisely the reverse—"non-zero-sum." For if the atomic bomb has taught us anything it surely is that either everyone gains or everyone loses, and thus sensible people pursue what that brilliant theorist of strategic bargaining Tom Schelling christened a "cooperative strategy."

The right-of-center view thus calls for more of precisely that which other critics of U.S. policy (and even Mr. Nixon) want to *reduce*—namely, intervention with unilateral U.S. military presence and power in local conflict situations around the world. Admiral Arleigh Burke ("30-knot Burke" of destroyer fame in World War II, now retired), who maneuvered lately with a fast-moving and prolific group of conservative strategic analysts at Georgetown University's Center for Strategic and International Studies, spoke for his side when he recently wrote:

> If there is no U.S. military presence to give these indigenous nations confidence *inevitably* they will feel the necessity of adjusting their policies to accommodate the only other major powers in the region, which in the near future will be the Soviet Union, and at some later date possibly Communist China. (*New York Times*, Op-Ed page, March 2, 1971)

I believe it is the word "inevitably" (which I underlined) that bothers me the most. As closed systems of belief and predetermined outcomes go, this seems to me to run Marxism a close second.

The military application of this philosophy calls for greatly increased expenditures in order to overcome what the American Security Council (a private hawkish group, not to be confused with the U.N. Security Council, which the right-wing deplores, or the President's National Security Council) has proclaimed to be a decisive Soviet lead over us in nuclear strength. The figures were controversial because the ASC in its publicity used as the measure of comparative strength *total deliverable "throw-weight"* —and the Russians do in fact have bigger bombs than we have. It is also true that Moscow made a successful drive to surpass the United States in number of land-based ICBM's, and soon will do so in nuclear-powered missile-firing subs (although remaining far behind in long-range bombers, nuclear-powered carriers, and other technology). Many people, however, including those in the Administration, believe that if you count up the number of *deliverable warheads* on each side, the lead is still heavily in our favor; and this evidently persuaded Mr. Nixon (whom no one could accuse of being soft on national security) to agree to freezing launcher levels in the 1972 SALT I agreement in a way that did give the Soviets a numerical advantage. (Senator Henry M. Jackson successfully pushed the Administration to try to equalize those gross numbers in SALT II.)

At the crucial political level, right-wing reality rests on a model of protracted political warfare between Communism—embodied in the Soviet state—and capitalist democracy, embodied in the United States of America. This implacable conflict is seen by them to persist regardless of Sino-Soviet splits, Titoism, or détente. In this sense, they mirror accurately the ideological purists on the Communist side who insist that détente is an aspect of unremitting ideological struggle. Indeed, the phrase "protracted war" was borrowed from Mao Tse-tung's writings by two of the chief American spokesmen for the conservative political-military view—Robert Strausz-Hupé and William Kintner, former directors of the Foreign Policy Research Institute in Philadelphia (and both named Ambassadors by President Nixon).

Many Americans share the militant right's repugnance with the inhumanities of Communist rule. Many Americans share their not unreasonable fear of the high cost of being wrong about Soviet motives and of what it takes to deter. But the difference lies in their refusal to modify the worldview formed at the height of the Cold War and to take the calculated risks aimed at sharply moderating the genocidal threat of warfare with today's weapons. As columnist Joseph Alsop expressed the position starkly:

> . . . this country, alone and foolishly guilt-ridden and confused by false councils, is literally all that stands between these hard-faced men and the rule of the whole world. This is what now places us in such a lonely and unknown situation. And that situation cannot be escaped. (*Boston Globe*, August 4, 1971)

Certain other foreign policy views much farther to the right can probably be best explained by a psychiatrist—as T. W. Adorno and his colleagues did brilliantly some years ago in a seminal book entitled *The Authoritarian Personality* (New York: Harper, 1950). It is evident that a fair number of Americans have to be both pacified and stimulated with martial sounds, flexed muscles, football metaphors, a sense of physical superiority, and occasional destructive acts against the fragile mechanism of international community such as the United Nations. Such Americans give the impression of entertaining a picture of reality more appropriate to endocrinology than diplomacy.

But how does one account for a trained lawyer such as Mr. Warren Richardson, general counsel of the right-wing action group Liberty Lobby, who paints the following surrealistic picture of what the world, including the U.S. private foundations, is like?

> These foundations [Ford, Rockefeller, Carnegie Endowment for International Peace, Council on Foreign Relations *et al.*] have long planned to socialize this world very quickly, by means of

wars, and by financing revolutionary projects—in this country and abroad—to distort and downgrade our American way of life. (*New York Times*, Op-Ed page, May 18, 1971)

What can anyone who knows the facts say to such a species of lunacy?

★ ★ ★ ★

The view from the left is a more complicated one. For one thing, it combines specific challenges to policy with varying degrees of alienation from the System itself. By definition, conservatives conserve the status quo, and radicals want change; and this is why most vocal and explicit critics of recent policy are found on the left. But both extremes are driven by ideology, and both feel alienated from the majority view. At their far extremes they approach each other, like the ends of a horseshoe: both the libertarians and the anarchists seek the virtual disappearance of the Federal Government.

At a more serious level they are of course deeply divided in their values. The rightists elevate personal autonomy and freedom—some would say license—to the highest value on the scale. The doctrinaire left idealizes a mass humanitarianism, organized along collectivist lines. The far right wants power to the strongest—including the strong and wealthy individual. The radical left wants power to the weakest—but with the *Lumpenproletariat* guided by an elite of sophisticated revolutionaries in the vanguard.

The left almost without exception thinks the notion of a Communist conspiracy is a myth contrived to justify U.S. expansion and intervention. The left says the United States was in Vietnam, if not for economic imperialism, then for field-testing the crushing of peasant revolutions. At its extreme—and this is what shook so many in the middle—the left was on the side of the Communists. Far from thinking the United States simply overextended or tactically misguided, the New Left is repelled by the "American way of life" and by policies to export it. In terms of collective security it finds the concept of the "free world" ludicrous. (In recent years I have had some trouble myself applying that phrase to some—but by no means all—places on "our side of the line.")

In theoretical terms, the New Left sees U.S. foreign policy as dominated by the pressures defined by Lenin in 1916 when he diagnosed imperialism as capitalism's drive to export capital, form monopolies, and divide up the world. From this springs the ultimate deduction that *all* U.S. foreign policy actions are motivated by "neo-imperialism." Their prescription for America is a socialist revolution at home, complete withdrawal of U.S. power and presence from abroad, and liquidation of U.S. overseas capital investments.

I am as troubled as the next person by the role of some private U.S. investments abroad, notably in Latin America, where they have had often deplorable effects on U.S.-Latin American relations, and in southern Africa, where they sometimes seem to underwrite a form of black slavery. The fantastic level of mass consumption achieved by U.S. society creates the anomaly that 6 per cent of the world's population consumes about 33⅓ per cent of its nonrenewable resources. This seems unjust and is unlikely to continue. But the underlying thesis of the radical left so distorts these problems as to be useless as diagnosis, let alone as prescription for cure.

The left destroys its basic credibility by its obsession with a single interpretation, given the many cases where the facts of American policy prove the opposite. It is almost enough to cite persistent support for Israel as against the enormous U.S. Middle East oil interests, which, according to the "economic imperialism" theory, should control U.S. policy. Another example was, of course, the Vietnam War, in which the entire monstrous U.S. investment has been without a single visible economic benefit in return—though of course the radical left was rescued from its embarrassed silence in the face of this fact by the discovery of offshore oil reserves near South Vietnam in the late 1960s.

The facts of American investments abroad do not in the main confirm the "imperialist" theory concerning U.S. involvement during the post-war years. For one thing, U.S. *exports*, important as they are to our balance of payments, still comprise only about 4 per cent of the total U.S. Gross National Product. *Two-thirds* of that 4 per cent goes, not to weak dependencies, but to high-income rich competitors. Private overseas *capital investment* is about $110 billion—a fraction of the two trillion-dollar total of U.S. investment—and the low-income countries see a declining percentage of it (currently around 33⅓).

Total U.S. overseas *investment income* is about $8 billion, as compared with some $80 billion from domestic operations of companies. Of this, a bit over $4 billion come from Third World countries, amounting to about 4 per cent of total U.S. GNP. Moreover, about 63 per cent of that is in *petroleum*, in which the producers now get the bulk of the proceeds. The rate of return on the remainder is substantially lower than before-taxes returns on investments in the U.S. As for U.S. dependence on *raw materials* from abroad, surely even the radical left has noticed how much leverage the producing countries are now exercising over the terms of the oil trade.

My Nobel Prize-winning M.I.T. associate Paul Samuelson spoke for most modern economists in writing that

> When Lenin and Rosa Luxemburg advanced the thesis of capitalism's dependence on outside markets for its prosperity, William Howard Taft was President and Maynard Keynes still a dilettante undergraduate at Cambridge. . . . The two fastest-growing mixed economies have been Germany and Japan—both stripped of their colonies and forbidden to have armies—which is empirical proof of Keynes' theoretical refutation of the imperialism thesis. (*New York Times*, October 30, 1970)

The almost hysterical American response to Castro's socializing (and subsequently Soviet-allied) revolution in Cuba, and President Johnson's convulsive occupation of Santo Domingo in 1965, were both echoes of an older imperialistic tradition that all too often found the U.S. Government lined up with the most undemocratic strongmen or oligarchies in the name of "stability." The chief fault of recent American policy, as I shall argue in more detail later, has been to make this deplorable phenomenon a world-wide one. In Latin America, more than any other region, it stemmed in large measure from private commercial interests, in addition to strategic concerns. And there is ample evidence that even a small investment can have disproportionate influence on a weak target country.

But we must be fair. American policy has changed considerably from the bad old days when private investments were defended with power and blood. In the 1920s when U.S. strategic and economic interests in the Caribbean or Central America seemed threatened, we landed the Marines. In 1968 when Peru nationalized the huge U.S.-owned International Petroleum Company holdings, we landed a New York lawyer named John Irwin, whose skill subsequently led him to be made Under Secretary of State and then Ambassador to France). When Fidel Castro adopted policies considered hostile to U.S. interests we severed relations. When Salvador Allende did the same in Chile a decade later we did little but frown—despite urging to action by the I.T.T. conglomerate. What kind of imperialism is that?

A particularly troubling element in the radical position is its ambiguity on the subject of violence. Here I have found some of the radical intellectuals quite inexcusable. For one thing, they have badly confused the young, who may not have understood strategy, but wept to see Indochinese civilians slaughtered by Americans with napalm and iron bombs, and insisted on reviving for us a desperately needed humanitarianism. But this valid corrective to our official dehumanizing became blurred when its extreme advocates also glorified and romanticized guerrillas terrorizing villages and selectively assassinating the leaders and teachers and public health nurses (as the Viet Cong did); kidnapping

A HOUSE DIVIDED

innocent victims for ransom (as the Tupamaros did); murdering peaceful tourists and athletes (as the Palestine Liberation groups did); burning and smashing innocent people's means of livelihood (as the Weathermen did)—all in the name of opposing oppression—and justified, as the well-known Norwegian "peace scholar" Johan Galtung argued on a lecture platform we recently shared in Vienna, on the ground that capitalist societies are themselves characterized by "structural violence."

This is a bloody and baffling phenomenon, this combination of abstract reasoning on peace alongside the condoning of personal violence. Thus, one idol of the New Left in Europe, Jean-Paul Sartre, was quoted as believing that "The intellectual who does not put his body as well as his mind on the line against the system is fundamentally supporting the system—and should be judged accordingly" (*New York Times Magazine*, October 17, 1971). In commenting on this the *Times*' William Shannon observed that "violence has always had a nervous fascination for many intellectuals."

> The masculine fantasies so evident in the writings of Hemingway and Mailer are clearly not an exclusively American daydream. Pale, bespectacled French intellectuals who lead outwardly passive lives also have dreams of testing their courage, of striding through the streets like heroes. Ordinary human beings would be safer if intellectuals left these crude, vulgar fantasies to Hollywood instead of projecting them on the world as political theories" (*New York Times*, October 21, 1971)

Eric Hoffer was everlastingly right, at least for the United States, when he warned that a true intellectual, once given political power, can become lethal to his fellow man. Herbert Marcuse, revered by a generation of young American radicals, preached the denial of civil rights to people with whom he disagrees; the name of that game is found in the title of a brilliant book by Israeli scholar J. L. Talmon, *The Rise of Totalitarian Democracy* (Boston: Beacon Press, 1952). Marcuse's position resembles in its intolerance that of the far right. A rightist intellectual who was originally a German Social Democrat, then a U.S. State Department official, later a consultant to the House Un-American Activities Committee, once urged publicly that free speech should be denied to the political left. Both are in the pernicious tradition established by Jean Jacques Rousseau when he wrote, "We shall force man to be free."

How does one square this with Thomas Jefferson's conviction—heretical when uttered—that if given some education, men can be trusted to govern themselves? Is there such a thing as too much education? Or is it a type of mind we should fear, the type whose "intellectual profile" should be posted at all political gatherings the way the hijacker's "personality profile" alerts the airline ticket agent? But of course the danger is not in intellectualism—i.e., the power of ideas, which we need as much of as possible to keep us rational. It is in the terrifying combination of intellectualism and political fanaticism. That alchemy creates people who bring to the subtle, fragile human equation the overpowering energy of a mind obsessed with abstractions about society. Add the component of militant action, and you have a mix that can be fatal to a nation that exists by compromise.

Communist-ruled countries (like Fascist régimes) are testimony to the pathology of power in the hands of fanatics. The point is not that they are Communists or Fascists. It is that they are fanatics. Ex-Communists who embrace another closed system of thought should be distrusted every bit as much as when they were using their special brand of intellectual-military judo on the soft mass of democracy. I am reminded of another acquaintance who tried to proselytize me to Communism when I was an undergraduate at Harvard. Mercifully I was turned off both by his mental rigidity and by the unbelievable dullness of *Das Kapital*. He happens to be a high government official today, still intolerant of error, even of questioning the line peddled in his agency's public prose.

It seems reasonable to suspect that where ravishing utopias combine with savage intolerance, there lurks a kind of madness. In his very last piece, the incomparable James Thurber, blind, dying, and frantically articulating some serious things he had subtly buried in his line drawings in the *New Yorker,* wrote:

> It isn't what the ideologist believes in, but what he hates, that puts the world in jeopardy. This is the force, in our time and in every other time, that urges the paranoic and the manic-depressive to become head of a state. Complete power not only corrupts but it also attracts the mad. (*"*The Future, If Any, of Comedy," *Harper's,* December 1961, p. 43)

★ ★ ★ ★

Despite my own rejection of both extremes, honesty compels the observation that the radical left, unlike the radical right, tends to recruit from among some of the most idealistic of our young people—those attracted to the preachers of humanitarianism rather than of selfish solutions. Outraged by their excesses, I still prefer the wrong-headed militant seekers after social justice to the hard-headed militant advocates of ever-increased power. The justice seeker is the dupe of a faulty theoretical prescription, but the power-hungry suffers from a deep confusion of human values. If we take as a guideline Francis Bacon's dictum that "truth emerges more readily from error than confusion," it seems to me that regardless of how distorted its analysis or inappropriate its remedies, the left, rather than the right, has focused on the worst unresolved problems in American society—and, within limits, in foreign policy as well.

Thus, the recruits to radicalism have shared with a much larger population of moderates some deeply-held beliefs of relevance to a better America. Failure to move the black American minority to equality faster, and less grudgingly, shocks them. They have heard all excuses, evolutionary programs, and statistics, but they still see the cancer of urban slums devouring millions of their fellow humans. What made Spiro Agnew a symbol of what is wrong with America was not necessarily the gusto with which he took his roundhouse swings—that is what makes American politics fun. It wasn't even his rather smug myopia. It was that he went out of his way to insult many Americans who were most concerned with the failure to solve the nation's toughest problems. Agnew is mercifully gone; but the problems remain.

The emotion of the young that should be valued the most, but one that foreign policy decision-making has tended to exclude from its calculations, is that of compassion. Illogical they may be, maddeningly selective in the victims of oppression they choose to support, obsessively focused on America's shortcomings. But to say those things cannot absolve the rest of us from accepting what is eternally right in their criticism, and glaringly missing from contemporary American foreign policy. Believing as I do that we need to restore compassion to an honored place in policy, I have to fault the young conservatives for missing this central point. (See for an egregious example 28-year-old Tom Charles Houston's advising President Nixon in 1971 that the F.B.I be subverted to crush Nixon's domestic political enemies.)

It is no answer to say, as the political right does, that others are cruel or calculating or inhuman. Nor is it an answer to say, as die-hard centrists do, that policy-makers and bureaucrats are at heart at least as humane and compassionate human beings as their critics. That was never the issue, at least with me. The issue is that the essential elements of human compassion and reverence for life (of other than Americans) have got filtered out of the process of decision-making. This has come about through a combination of the bureaucratic consensus process, and the institutionalization of power-type responses to international crises. That combination justified primarily military and *Realpolitik* responses to external events, and eventually produced a distorted caricature of the proper U.S. world role and image.

I do not for a minute expect or want U.S. foreign policy to rest on pure sentiment or unalloyed humanitarianism. The world is much too hard a place for that. But I do want our middle-aged decision-makers to try harder to get the feel (which they rarely do) of the frame of mind and heart our hopelessly sentimental, idealistic young people tried so hard in recent times to communicate. Perhaps then their elders and betters will still say such half-valid things as "You can't help everyone," or "Aerial bombing is most cost-effective," or "Don't you want to be able to get a security clearance when you grow up?" or even "Why aren't you ever as concerned with Communism's victims?" But it is also possible that the readmission of compassion into the hard-nosed councils of state will prove itself most "cost-effective" of all in making Americans feel comfortable once again with their world role.

Although it is true that campus turmoil was generally engineered by only a tiny fraction of the student body, *the majority of seemingly inert students was basically in sympathy with the general goals and concerns of the radicals.* This was the overwhelming fact, and the great reason the Nixon-Agnew rhetoric about "campus bums" and "a few rotten apples" was so misplaced. It is not that there were no bums and rotten apples. It is that, particularly in the 1968–70 dissent, while only fifty youths would show up for a rally about working conditions in college kitchens, or "U.S. imperialism in Latin America," or Vietnam, just let the cops come in and bust the shaggy heads of the radicals, and the rest would be out by the thousands, striking, rallying, cursing authority, and in many cases "becoming radicalized." The evidence for this phenomenon was overwhelming on campus after campus. It should have been—but was not—obvious to every professional in the "stability" business that it was *not* simply a matter of "getting rid of a few troublemakers" (or "outside agitators," as white Southerners so long characterized those who came and stirred up the otherwise ecstatically happy slumdwellers segregated under Jim Crow laws). It was that the majority also turned out to care.

Some of the young were, as ever, just plain glandular. In 1937 on a May evening when the moon was high and the air like wine we all poured out into Harvard Yard from our freshman dorms, and some began breaking windows and a few even hit cops. Some also marched on real pre-war issues such as U.S. intervention *versus* U.S. isolationism. In the more recent campus brouhahas there were some for whom shouting, marching, and even "trashing" was simply more purgative than sitting hunched over a book, or yearning for a beautiful physical relationship. This feature of dissent should make people leery of the sort of adulation of the youth culture advocated as a secular solution by Charles Reich in *The Greening of America*.

But others were putting their money where their mouths were. With empathy they were acting out the behavior specified by one of their intellectual heroes, a French writer with phenomenal influence on many young Americans. The late Albert Camus reached them deeply with his insight that rebellion is possible *even if one's own interests are not involved*. It is hard to imagine an ethical position so diametrically opposed to the "I've Got Mine, Jack" attitude that seemed to characterize the newly affluent middle class virtually everywhere. The two positions symbolized an ethical conflict immemorially present wherever a Pharisee crosses to the other side to avoid a beggar or a leper, or a social problem that isn't directly damaging to one's interests. "Why rebel if there is nothing worth preserving in oneself?" Camus asked an audience that was more than ready for his words.

> The slave asserts himself for the sake of everyone in the world when he comes to the conclusion that a command has infringed on something inside him that does not belong to him alone, but which he has in common with other men—even with the man who insults and oppresses him. . . . Then we note that *revolt does not occur only amongst the oppressed but that it can break out at the mere spectacle of oppression of which someone else is the victim.* (*The Rebel*, 1965, p. 22; italics mine)

★ ★ ★ ★

I have to conclude that the radical critique of *neither* American political extreme represents a useful set of economic, social, or military policies for the nation, even though both have pieces of the truth that we disregard at our peril. Both push for changes in policy that go beyond any limits recognizable to the great majority of people who live in the United States. It has been shown again and again that the American majority simply will not accept either their diagnoses or their detailed prescriptions. As Professor Sidney Hook once noted, what is needed is a peace movement with an unambiguous commitment to the cause of human freedom (*New York Times Magazine*, October 13, 1963). It is also profoundly true that the trouble with many conservatives is that they do not understand democracy, while the trouble with many liberals is that they do not understand Communism.

The Greek poet Archilochus wrote that "The fox knows many things, but the hedgehog knows one big thing." The revolutionary hedgehog is in possession of one large idea with seductive power—an idea that gains him adherents who yearn for once-for-all solutions. But as a guide to national policy—at least for this nation—this is medicine that if taken straight can destroy us. Life is far too complex to allow fanatics to run it for us. On the right hand, because a society based on hate, greed, and naked power is too much like Thomas Hobbes' state of nature from which civilized man must flee; on the left hand, because of its disabling alienation, its attachment to oversimplified solutions, its neurotic idolatry of youth, its permanent passion for dissent, and at the limits its advocacy of civil violence. "My country, right or left" (as W. N. Medlicoff put it) is not good enough grounds for patriotism, at least for me.

To the extent that some calls for revolution are largely rhetorical, their failure is pungently explained by that old Bolshevik Nikita Khrushchev, who said while still in power that "If you feed people just with revolutionary slogans, they will listen today, they will listen tomorrow, they will listen the day after tomorrow, but on the fourth day they will say 'The hell with you' " (At a Kremlin reception September 19, 1964).

Indeed, the relevant lessons were drawn by the genuine revolutionaries of the past. All utopians ought to remember Danton's sad reflection that "revolution devours its children." They should have read enough Communist literature to know what Friedrich Engels wrote of the 1871 Paris Commune, in his Introduction to Marx's *Civil War in France*: ". . . the irony of history willed—as is usual when doctrinaires come to the helm—that both did the opposite of what the doctrines of their school prescribed" (*Engels: Selected Writings* [London: Penguin, 1967], p. 307). And the bizarre coalition of left and right who unite on anarchism need to take to heart Albert Camus' conclusion that "All modern revolutions have ended in reinforcement of state power."

But the dilemma for the United States is that, even if the extremists repel us, we still have to make major changes if we are to restore our national spirit. We have to redefine our values, and as we redefine them so we must redefine our foreign policy. I fear that the needful changes will *not* come if we fail to extract such truths as are buried in the radical critique; and in this sense the extremists always have an indispensable role in major reform. They are highly misleading to take seriously as physicians able to heal a sick body. But without them there will be no cutting edge to the diffuse sense that change is needed.

DIAGNOSIS

★ 3 ★

THE CRUMBLING CONSENSUS

The Establishment

Many critics of the state of American society or the direction of U.S. foreign policy in recent times agree upon indicting the "Establishment" for the evils of both. The Establishment ran the Government, owned the money, invented the conventional wisdom, and put down the poor, the young, and the minorities—so the argument went.

At the apex of this elite presumably were found those who direct our affairs, and at *their* head was the President of the United States—or at least so I thought until President Nixon told *Times*-man C. L. Sulzberger "Frankly, I have more confidence in our people than in the Establishment" (*New York Times*, March 10, 1971). The confusion doubtless arose from Mr. Nixon's perennial (and probably justified) resentment of the so-called "Eastern Establishment," that allegedly sinister and powerful combination of Wall Street bankers, foundation philanthropoids, Lower Manhattan law firms, and a few select universities. Senator Barry Goldwater was so dismayed at the power wielded by this coterie of "effete snobs" (to use the label later applied by Spiro Agnew) that in his 1964 Presidential campaign he spoke of sawing off the Eastern seaboard and floating it out to sea.

The significant point, however, is that Mr. Nixon and virtually all national political figures were enthusiastic participants in the American coalition that for three decades fostered the dominant U.S. internationalist, interventionist foreign policies. These may have been devised with the help of the Eastern Establishment, but they were for years nation-wide in constituency.

This was the set of policies on which the nation formed a long-term consensus. This was the stance and role I have labeled the "liberal approach." This was the approach I am arguing has become in certain ways defective, deficient, and even dangerous, but which has still not been adequately diagnosed, nor have appropriate remedies been prescribed for its ills.

★ ★ ★ ★

Two aspects characterized this general approach and the consensus that supported it: the *people* centrally involved in it, and the *set of beliefs* that drove it as a program for action on the world scene. The people are important because the left argues that U.S. foreign policy is a class affair, explainable not only by the imperialist quest for markets and raw materials but also by elite dominance in the context of class struggle.

This paradigm has had an extraordinary appeal to younger Americans who are not necessarily Marxists but to whom U.S. policies have looked increasingly sordid. What more seductive explanation than the financial holdings and social backgrounds of the middle-aged men running the State Department, the Pentagon, the CIA, and the Council on Foreign Relations? What more plausible villain than the giant corporations which, armed with the power of the Government, their rationale supplied by the captive intellectuals, could oppress the peoples of the Third World?

In a book entitled *The Roots of American Foreign Policy* (Boston: Beacon Press, 1969), Gabriel Kolko, one of the most probing of the so-called revisionist historians, captioned a chapter "The Men of Power." He reported his research on what he called the "career cycles" and origins of key American foreign policy "decision-makers" from 1944 to 1960, excluding the Presidents: a group of 234 individuals holding 678 government posts, "nearly all of them high level and policy-making in nature." Kolko's findings were

> that foreign policy decision-makers are in reality a highly mobile sector of the American corporate structure, a group of men who frequently assume and define high level policy tasks in government, rather than routinely administer it, and then return to business. Their firms and connections are large enough to afford them the time to straighten out or formulate government policy while maintaining their vital ties with giant corporate law, banking, or industry. The conclusion is that a small number of men fill the large majority of key foreign policy posts. Their many diverse posts make this group a kind of committee government entrusted to handle numerous and varied national security and international functions at the policy level. Even if not initially connected with the corporate sector, career government officials relate in some tangible manner with the private worlds predominantly of big law, big finance, and big business. (P. 17)

His conclusion, in simplified form, was that the content of U.S. foreign policy correlates directly with the social class and financial interests of this group, along with U.S. culpability for the Cold War.

As with much of the revisionist findings, this contains germs of a sobering truth. Also as typical of the genre, however, it uses the facts to support a devil theory in which U.S. policies toward both Communism and the Third World are explained by the empowerment of men from such suspect backgrounds.

This is what makes it so hard to put to good use the insights developed by the revisionists. They teach some very illuminating things about the early post-war period—things one either didn't realize at the time or misremembers—although they all tend to commit the crucial error of imputing to the United States of 1945 the Cold War posture and attitudes of 1947 and later. There was, as any one involved at the time knows, a world of difference between the two. This is important because, by moving 1947 back to 1945, they claim to "prove" that the United States was responsible for initiating the Cold War, which is what revisionism wants to prove. The trouble comes when they insist on a package deal: the theory must go with the facts. This causes them to have to play down or even leave out facts that inconveniently undermine the theory.

The whole problem of scholarship is of course vastly simplified if one can explain history in terms of hidden plots. But try as I will, I cannot make it all fit, and am forced to conclude that Mr. Kolko and his ilk have tumbled into the old logical fallacy of *post hoc ergo propter hoc*. In other words, since the policies of the Cold War period set in *after* the arrival in government of many volunteers from business, banking, and law firms, it follows that those policies were the *result* of their presence.

I am fully prepared to believe that some among the McCloys and Dulleses and Achesons and Lovetts and Harrimans and Lodges and Rusks and Dillons and Bundys and McCones (to mention a few leaders of the named elite) brought into government the snobbery of their respective backgrounds or the self-confidence of inherited wealth, and in all cases the conviction that free private enterprise and the secret ballot were preferable to state Socialism and uncontested elections. But just to jog everybody's thinking, how about a different hypothesis, a *propter hoc ergo post hoc?* Rather than that their services *caused* the whole thing, what if the onset of virulent political warfare between the two ideological/power systems, accompanied by acute international security threats plus a massive U.S. response, was what convinced men like these that their services were needed and would be appreciated?

After all, not many Wall Street tycoons and Republican lawyers flocked into Washington during the New Deal years in order to take over the nation. But from 1945 to 1960, because the times seemed to be calling forth a militant-cum-charitable American response, the men to whom this mix appealed interrupted their lucrative private work to join the Government as they had done in wartime. At least, this seems equally plausible as a theory.

This leads to an even greater weakness of the elitist-conspiracy theory. To make its point, this theory has to premise that the individuals in question are policy-makers; if they are not, then of course there is no case. This is a problem I have with my students and my inexperienced academic colleagues, most of whom fall into the easy habit of referring to anyone above the level of desk officer in Washington as a policy-maker. There is only one real policy-maker, at least in modern times. This is the President (who, by the way, is the only one so authorized by the Constitution, which makes no reference to the Secretary of State or any other official). In fact one of the central issues in the debate on foreign policy is the increasing monopoly by the man in the White House over basic policy on the really important matters (e.g., Europe, the Middle East, SALT, or China). As anyone on the Senate Foreign Relations Committee will be glad to point out, both the elected members of the Congress *and* most senior policy officials appointed by the President to advise him have more and more been ignored, disregarded, or overridden. That Mr. Kolko's sample survey of "backgrounds" omits the President is reason enough to wonder about the validity of his conclusions.

On the other hand, according to former Air Force Under Secretary Townsend Hoopes in his critique of U.S.-Vietnam policy-making entitled *The Limits of Intervention* (New York: David McKay, 1969), the inner "National Security Elite" by virtue of its shared premises often could influence the President to move in directions desired also by outside critics who were *not* in the center because of being either the wrong age, social class, or ideological persuasion, and thus not acceptable sources of serious advice.

A vigorous attempt to refute the Kolko-type thesis was made by a man who until recently worked in the very heart of what I must for the moment again call the Establishment (since both Kolko and his refuter do). As managing editor of the quarterly *Foreign Affairs*, Philip Quigg had a matchless opportunity to examine at close quarters the many hundreds of people who made up the influential Eastern group that filters through the portals of the Council on Foreign Relations and the pages of its journal. Writing in unabashed justification of much U.S. policy of the post-war period, Quigg has a different impression of the elite. "No country in the world," he says, "lends itself so poorly to the Establishment concept as the United States. Not only are the sources of power here more diversified, but geographically they are scattered as nowhere else and becoming more so all the time." He points out that the most powerful men in the Congress are not even on the fringes of the Establishment, most coming from rural areas of the South and Southwest; and that even the Cabinet is short of Establishment figures. His own picture of the ruling group is nothing short of ecumenical:

> Doubtless a member of the New Left or the John Birch Society would find in the group a certain homogeneity, for the spectrum of opinion represented has limits which are unacceptable to either one. To almost anyone else, the range would seem wide indeed—inevitably so, composed as the group is of scholars and men of affairs, of bankers and civil servants, of labor leaders and Congressmen, of young men and old. About all that they may be said to have in common is an interest in international affairs, a belief that the United States has a role to play in those affairs, and a bias in favor of orderly change. Some believe that the United States (Vietnam aside) is overcommitted abroad; others feel that extensive involvement is inevitable or salutary or both. Some believe that private enterprise not only is good at home but is the only way that the Third World will lift itself out of poverty; others be-

lieve that a large element of socialism is necessary and are often highly critical of American business abroad. Almost all believe in international cooperation; virtually none believes world government is feasible, but many would consider it a desirable, if distant, objective. (*America the Dutiful* [New York: Simon & Schuster, 1971], p. 181)

My final problem with the revisionist description of the Establishment is with the use of old statistics. Ending his 1969 survey as of 1960 made it impossible for Mr. Kolko to deal with the very period when the consensus began springing leaks, the time when members of the inner group themselves often became the critics.

A rather more revealing statistic concerns the social and class origins of the American Foreign Service. Bankers and Wall Street lawyers come in to do a job the President or the Congress decides should be done, and then they go. But the bureaucracy goes on forever, and the tone *it* sets can be far more enduring. I used to worry that the U.S. Foreign Service, like Harvard College, undermined its own innate excellence (I admit bias) by seeming to imprint a fairly uniform air of stuffiness and arrogance that so often made them (us) look absurd. But while Harvard has in some ways blended into the proletarian uniformity of the contemporary college scene, the Foreign Service mentality, like that of all elite career services, still tends at times to be its own worst enemy. Even so, some other statistics as to its sociology should be sobering to the devil theorist:

> Prior to 1925, 64 percent of all American diplomats had attended Harvard, Yale, or Princeton. By 1936-1939, these three schools were providing 26 percent of new recruits into the Foreign Service, a figure which fell to 15 percent for the years 1957-1962 and 9 percent in 1969-1970. Of the 103 new Foreign Service officers in 1969-1970, 24 of them attended Ivy League schools as undergraduates. (The late John Franklin Campbell, in *The Foreign Affairs Fudge Factory* [New York: Basic Books, 1971], p. 120)

The truth of the matter can probably be better found on a historical rather than a sociological basis. Having worked closely with many of the people who helped tend the foreign policy machine over the last twenty-five years, it seems to me that the overwhelming fact about them (us) was the picture the generation in power carried in its heads about the nature of reality.

The men in power—and most attentive Americans not in power—for years shared a number of cardinal convictions about how the world operates. These convictions were shaped in the crucible of World War II, where the memories of democracy's failure to oppose aggression in the 1930s and the experience of the ensuing violence combined to produce a new amalgam the likes of which America had never seen before. It was well described by Townsend Hoopes in his engrossing inside story of the bureaucracy's agonizing over Vietnam:

> Like everyone else in the United States over forty, the President's advisers were children of the Cold War in the sense that their thinking about world strategy and world politics had been decisively shaped by that phenomenon. Still relatively young and impressionable when they emerged from the wholesale fighting of World War II, they had found that the fruit of victory was a bitter bipolar enmity stretching around the globe, and apparently restrained from the plunge into final holocaust only by a delicate balance of terror. They had lived in this political-military frame of iron for the better part of twenty years, urgently preoccupied with mortal struggle against a formidable Communist structure. (*The Limits of Intervention*, p. 9)

In other words, in the 1940s and 1950s the global-scale crises generated by Stalinist policy in Eastern Europe and elsewhere, together with the U.S. determination to resist it, were appropriately dealt with by a model based on traumatic memories of American abstention from responsibility, appeasement of unappeasable aggressors, and failure to develop collective security machinery. But what drove the early post-war American Cold Warrior was very rarely, if ever, a dream of crushing Communism or fostering American investments. The first was not much considered (except by such dubiously balanced individuals as Bertrand Russell, who, twenty years before he demanded war crimes trials for U.S. leaders, called for a preventive nuclear war against the Soviet Union). The second collapses in the face of the unprecedented U.S. rehabilitation of its prime commercial competitors, Western Europe and Japan. As Jean Laloy wrote in *Foreign Affairs*, "It is an odd form of imperialism which is blind enough to create its own rival" ("Does Europe Have a Future?" October 1972, pp. 154–66). In addition there were policies such as land reform in occupied Japan which, according to a critical British observer, "freed Japan in perpetuity from dictation by a landowning elite" ("American Quarter Century in Asia," by Dick Wilson, *Foreign Affairs*, July 1973, pp. 811–30).

Having said all that, one can freely concede a whole congeries of faults, stupidities, prejudices, ideological sets, and outmoded beliefs, many of which still linger on to damage U.S. foreign policy. Just so long as no one continues to insist that it was all a plot by Wall Street (which was, in fact, one of the most influential voices against continuing the Vietnam War).

Premises and Preconceptions

What were the great majority of Americans *for* in the post-war years? What did the conventional wisdom about U.S. foreign policy really consist of? What assumptions did it rest on?

It may be instructive to list the premises that seem to lie beneath the foreign policy consensus as it took shape in the late 1940s. Obviously, some are no longer believed by most people in the so-called foreign policy community. Just as obviously, some are still valid to many people (including myself), and deserve to be believed. Others were appropriate to the 1950s and early 1960s and may or may not retain validity. Others of these premises may be dubious indeed, but are still shared, consciously or unconsciously, by people in the community, particularly inside govern-

•

ment. In retrospect I would contend even that some of these dubious assumptions were *never* really valid, and caused great damage to America and sometimes to other peoples as well.

Not all—perhaps not any—are original with me. But even those that have been rehashed elsewhere are included in the list, since it is not yet proved that whatever challenges they have met within the system have been sharp enough to clarify what it is we have been doing in the world, and why.

Here, then, is the list:

1. Communism is bad; capitalism is good. (Haven't practically all Americans believed this?)

2. Stability is desirable; in general, instability threatens U.S. interests. (Despite some efforts to put the United States on the anti-status quo side, this premise overwhelmingly underlies U.S. policy actions toward the Third World since the 1950s.)

3. Democracy (our kind, that is) is desirable, but if a choice has to be made, stability serves U.S. interests better than democracy. (This expresses the chief political, moral, and spiritual problem of our foreign policy.)

4. Any area of the world that "goes socialist" or neutralist is a net loss to us, and probably a victory for the Soviets. (Despite Tito, the box-score mentality long dominated U.S. post-war policy and still may, even though the political balances have profoundly shifted.)

5. Every country, and particularly the poor ones, would benefit from American "know-how." (One of our greatest shocks was to learn that we frequently don't know how when it comes to reshaping other cultures.)

6. Nazi aggression in the 1930s and democracy's failure to respond provides the appropriate model for dealing with post-war security problems. (The trouble came in distinguishing genuine Hitler-type threats to the global order from a miscellany of civil wars, revolutions, subversion, nationalism, and social change.)

7. Allies and clients of the United States, regardless of their political structure, are members of the Free World. (This may be no more than rhetoric, but it is still employed by many in government who can no longer define it without embarrassment.)

8. Western Europe (a) is indefensible without something like

the current U.S. military presence and (b) would not be defended by the people who live there, for the reason that (c) they don't understand the threat or haven't the will to stand up to it. (Our European allies have encouraged us to believe this, but the threat is increasingly hard to define, and the Europeans are surely intelligent enough to define their interests when we inevitably reduce our military presence.)

9. The United States must provide leadership because it (reluctantly) has the responsibility. (While obviously valid on some counts, this one has fallen from grace as a universal principle but is still believed by many, including Richard Nixon in his second Inaugural.)

10. The United States has vital interests in (a) the Pacific and (b) some or (c) all of the offshore Asian territories, and (d) some parts of the Asian mainland. (Easy to show but hard to analyze.)

11. "Modernization" and "development" are good for poor, primitive, or traditional societies—and they will probably develop into democracies by these means. (The first hypothesis, like the quest for economic growth, is vulnerable on spiritual grounds; the second on the evidence is increasingly dubious.)

12. Foreign aid (a) rests on an altruistic concern for the wellbeing of others, (b) should inspire gratitude and pro-U.S. feelings, (c) is only justifiable if it promotes specific U.S. interests. (Phrased this way to illustrate our schizoid approach to foreign assistance, which, since it does neither (b) or (c), needs redefinition on forthright humanitarian grounds.)

13. In international negotiation the United States has a virtual monopoly on "sincerity." (Americans since Ben Franklin have believed this, at least until recently.)

14. Violence is an unacceptable way to secure economic, social, and political justice—except when vital U.S. interests are at stake. (Most Americans admire the English and American revolutions of 1688 and 1776 but deplore those of Russia and China in 1917 and 1949.)

15. Depending on the extent to which U.S. interests are at stake, the United Nations is either the noblest hope of mankind, or a nuisance. (Is more evidence really needed for this proposition?)

16. The world should live under international law (but the

United States will neither repeal the Connally Reservation, which undercut the International Court, nor ratify the Genocide Convention, which we persuaded the United Nations to pass in 1948).

17. In Southern Africa the United States favors racial equality but not at the price of (a) instability or (b) economic loss. (Not necessarily hypocrisy; rather, a policy premise with an irreconcilable internal inconsistency.)

18. Incipient foreign conflicts warrant top-level U.S. attention only when they threaten to become violent. When they become acute, only diplomatic and military considerations are relevant. (If this isn't true, why does U.S. decision machinery spring into action only when violence threatens, and why is the NSC exclusively political-military in make-up?)

19. However egregious a mistake, the Government must never admit having been wrong. (Eisenhower acknowledging the U-2 spy flight is the only example of admitting wrong-*doing*. No one admits having *been* wrong.)

20. Challenging underlying assumptions such as these is "speculative," "theoretical," and a one-way ticket out of the inner policy circle. (Read a few memoirs. Ask why the Policy Planning Staff is a shadow of its former self.)

If at one time a full consensus existed on these propositions, either on conscious or unconscious levels, it has substantially crumbled so far as many in the foreign policy community are concerned. But a number of these articles of belief are still reflected both in U.S. policies and in the arguments made by defenders of the policy status quo. Perhaps the one that kept the ensemble of premises coherent for so long was the belief, reaffirmed by the late President Lyndon B. Johnson, that "if the United States abandoned its responsibilities" no one would "pick them up."

> As I had said in 1956, we did not ask to be the guardians at the gate, but there was no one else. There was no question in my mind that the vacuum created by our abdication would be filled inevitably by the Communist powers. (*The Vantage Point: Perspectives on the Presidency, 1963–1969* [New York: Holt, Rinehart & Winston, 1971], p. 422–23)

THE CRUMBLING CONSENSUS

Much of U.S. policy was right for the period 1945 to the early 1960s, and, despite the revisionists, was so recognized by virtually the entire non-Communist world. It is still worth the dogged (and often hopeless) effort to teach young Americans to understand where the United States has been right as well as wrong. Only those who neither remember nor want to learn can ignore the immensely different circumstances in the years when practically every non-Communist, and some Communist, countries appealed to the United States for help and leadership against the threats of their dissolution or extinction.

The trouble came in believing, two decades later, that nothing had changed. As former Under Secretary of State George Ball wrote in 1971, our partners expect of us "that finally, we will reassert that calm, firm leadership that has served the world so well for the past three decades" (*Newsweek*, November 29, 1971). This same worldview was spelled out by Freedom House, a centrist American organization dedicated to world-wide freedom—plus steadfast anti-Communism. A statement published in December 1970, signed by forty leading Establishment figures in business, public affairs, and intellectual circles, concluded with the following statement:

> . . . the United States has a clear call to continuing leadership in world affairs. This is not a role it chose. It was chosen by events. America now has no real choice in abdicating this role; it has the choice only between fulfilling and defaulting its responsibilities to free men and free institutions, and to future generations. (*Freedom at Issue*, January/February, 1971, p. 5)

In other words, despite everything that has happened, the United States retains a unique mandate to lead the non-Communist world. I for one do not believe it. I do, however, believe that policies of greater co-operation and economic equity will meet a warm response; and if we want to call that "leadership" or being "Number One," that's perfectly all right with me.

Those with short memories for history might well ponder the

durable theme of a supernatural calling for this nation. It was not an invention of power-drunk Cold Warriors, nor even of those turn-of-the-century imperialists intoxicated with the heady wine of overseas empire. Rather, it goes back to the very birth of this nation and even earlier. For almost three hundred years the theme has recurred of a unique, even divine, American world role. The Puritan Jonathan Edwards claimed that Providence intended America to be the renovator of the world, and George Washington's Farewell Address announced that "It will be worthy of a free, enlightened . . . Nation to give to mankind the magnanimous and too novel example of a people guided by an exalted justice and benevolence."

John Adams in a moment of political ecstasy wrote to Jefferson in 1813 that "Our pure, virtuous, public-spirited, federative republic, will last forever, govern the globe, and introduce the perfection of man." Practical politician Henry Clay said that the American contribution to freedom was to keep "the lamp burning brightly on this western shore, as a light to all nations."

The universal theme was sounded by Abraham Lincoln, who said that the Declaration of Independence "gave liberty not alone to the people of this country, but hope to all the world, for all future time." So R. W. Emerson called America "a beacon lighting for all the world the paths of human destiny."

Over seventy years ago Richard Olney, Grover Cleveland's Secretary of State, summarized U.S. traditions of altruism:

> The people of the United States have a vital interest in the cause of popular self-government. . . . They believe it to be for the healing of all nations, and that civilization must either advance or retrograde as its supremacy is extended or curtailed.

In his more flamboyant rhetoric Theodore Roosevelt declaimed

> We, here in America, hold in our hands the hope of the world, the fate of the coming years; and shame and disgrace will be ours if in our eyes the light of high resolve is dimmed, if we trail in the dust the golden hopes of men.

THE CRUMBLING CONSENSUS

The spirit of the Puritan divine emerged in Woodrow Wilson's proclamation that America's world responsibilities and mission had come "by no plan of our conceiving, but by the hand of God who led us this way." That same pietistic figure, President Wilson, who influenced the Democratic Party, John Foster Dulles, and even Richard Nixon, went perhaps farther than anyone in denying self-interest to America:

> It is a very perilous thing to determine the foreign policy of a nation in the terms of material interest. . . . We dare not turn from the principle that morality and not expediency is the thing that must guide us. . . . We have no selfish ends to serve. . . . We are but one of the champions of the right of mankind.

In our own age the identical theme continued to be sounded. The Herter Committee Report, on which the foreign aid program came to be based, trumpeted that "our Nation is commissioned by history to be either an observer of freedom's failure or the cause of its success."

President Kennedy in 1961 ascribed to this country the role of "watchman on the walls of freedom" assigned to us by destiny. And President Nixon placed himself squarely in the same tradition of reluctant, altruistically-motivated responsibility when he told an interviewer that

> no one who is really for peace . . . can reject an American role in the rest of the world. . . . We had fought four wars, selflessly and for no gain. . . . Our responsibilities are not limited to this great continent. . . . [The Communist leaders] are . . . thankful that the United States wants nothing—nothing but the right for everyone to live and let live. (Interview with C. L. Sulzberger, *New York Times*, March 10, 1971)

This strain in American belief and rhetoric strikes a jarring note today. It combines an embarrassing self-righteousness with what the political philosopher Raymond Aron (speaking, incidentally, of Karl Marx) called "catastrophic optimism." Yet this nation in fact *did* furnish a beacon for many people, and it *did* provide a model for new democracies, and for generations it *was* unself-seeking in its relations with others.

Nevertheless, much else about the world has seemed to change in our times, and America's place in that world is no exception.

Cold War Hang-ups

Policy attitudes can in the end best be understood by where one stands along a single but fundamental dimension. It is this: How do you view Communism, the Soviet Union, and what Pentagon staff documents used to call "The Nature of the Threat" arising from one or both? The answers tell a good deal about whether one is focused primarily on internal or external relations; whether one believes the United States should execute a major or a minor withdrawal from global involvement; and the extent to which the United States does or does not still carry a special "responsibility" and must still exercise "leadership" in its world role. For of all the other nations in the world, only the Soviet Union has the power to destroy the United States and the rest of the planet.

American interpretations of Soviet Communism's threat to world peace and to the independence of certain nations were widely shared in the period 1945–55. Few problems of interpretation were raised by a world in ruins and menaced by starvation as well as capture by small but highly organized bands of conspirators. These conspirators at least in Eastern Europe were backed by the bayonets of the Red Army, loyally took their orders from Moscow, and had received no recognizable mandate from the people they proposed to rule. Far from plotting to invent trouble with Russia in order to win economic domination of the world (as argued by some revisionist historians), the evidence is overwhelming that America was profoundly shocked to discover after World War II that instead of resuming its uninvolved national life in the new world of law and order under the U.N. Charter, it confronted chaos, collapse, and the age-old specter of a big power on the move

THE CRUMBLING CONSENSUS

to exploit weakness in order to expand its influence and reach, as well as gain security.

The American assumption of responsibility to help rebuild Europe and to aid countries disrupted by the war was of course self-interested; but it was also altruistic. So was wartime Lend-Lease, which Winston Churchill called "the most unsordid act in history." Few apart from the most incorrigible America-haters at home and abroad have denied American unselfishness in either case. Indeed, the later result of rebuilding its principal commercial competitors—Western Europe and Japan—was deep financial and economic problems for this country; but those costs were earlier faced and accepted in the name of a cause that simply could not be explained by the Marxist hypothesis about imperialism.

Beneath the surface, however, the straightforward Cold War lineup was irrevocably loosening up. The issues could no longer be defined in undifferentiated terms of "us" or "them." The Communists themselves helped to obscure the changes taking place. Many Westerners took their counterinsurgency cue from Soviet Premier Khrushchev's January 1961 speech supporting "wars of national liberation" (but rejecting general and limited ones), and from Chinese Defense Minister Lin Piao's 1963 metaphor of the countryside surrounding and annihilating the "cities" (but elliptically warning Hanoi that it could not count on Chinese troops). That both turned out to be more rhetoric than policy was in turn obscured by some lingering Soviet bluster about Berlin, by Chinese internal convulsions, and by unchecked rivalry in the Middle East.

But while change was arriving, the post-war U.S. role of crusader and rescuer had acquired a momentum that carried it into a historic period in which many of its underlying presumptions were no longer valid. As early as the mid-1950s Stalin and many aspects of Stalinism were dead; long-range nuclear weapons delivery systems made all countries physically vulnerable; and a whole new world was wakening in the southern hemisphere. By the mid-

1960s Russia and China were virtually at war, and evidence was mounting that the Third World was not going to be anyone's, neither "theirs" nor "ours." If it was absurd when in 1956 Anthony Eden compared Nasser with Hitler, it was equally unconvincing in the 1960s, when Dean Rusk persistently used the model of the Saar, Sudetenland, and Munich to explain U.S. policy in Indochina despite the vastly different setting, background, and motives underlying the efforts to take power.

My main point here is that the contemporary crisis in U.S. foreign policy had its first great source in the attempt to transfer to the Third World the formulas and strategic concepts of the grim post-war confrontation with dynamic Soviet power. The application of Cold War doctrines to fundamentally different situations produced a series of contentious policies reaching a climax in the protracted and increasingly inhumane U.S. involvement in Vietnam, the consequences of which we have not yet fully sorted out.

Meanwhile, America's unresolved domestic problems, above all racial, were reaching critical mass. The escalating Vietnam War was the trigger that set off the chain reaction.

The third paramount event was the spectacular détente policy of the Soviet Union under Leonid Brezhnev, culminating in the Moscow summit of May 1972, and the Brezhnev visit to the United States in June 1973, complete with the announcement that the détente process was "irreversible."

From this combination of external change and internal combustion, many Americans have based their prescriptions for policy change on the assumption that even if it had ever existed, the basic Soviet "threat" has disappeared. They argue that Moscow's attitude toward the U.S. has changed profoundly, and that the Cold War should thus be regarded as a thing of the past. Others, however, warn that the threat remains, and fear disaster for America from what they see as dangerous illusions arising from détente, SALT agreements, and the warm embrace of American eagle with Russian bear. They point out that the Soviet Union is still a

THE CRUMBLING CONSENSUS

totalitarian and repressive society, still fundamentally hostile to the West, and still capable of international perfidy. Some of these Americans believe that the Soviets threaten us by spreading their naval power and their search for influence around the world; others, however, hold that they are acting just as Germany and the United States acted at the turn of the century in order to catch up with Britain as a great power).

President Nixon's brilliant summitry conveyed a welcome message that the two superpowers could improve their relations. Meanwhile, the Nixon Defense Department acted as though the military threat were unchanged; and in the country at large there was far less serious discussion of the underlying premises than in preceding periods. Thus, the prime question about foreign policy continued to be dealt with by vague and subjective assertions that "the Cold War is over" or "the Cold War is not over"; the crucial national debate about priorities and policies has been staged with astonishingly little attention to the most important element in the equation, except in moments of crisis such as the renewed Arab-Israeli War in 1973.

Worse still is the tendency to choose up sides on this issue and thus not see the ambiguities that characterize it. It is sadly predictable that most who believe in one interpretation of Soviet behavior tend to rule out other interpretations that are equally plausible, given the evidence. Thus, some who believe that détente is a good thing and want to encourage it seem unable to believe also that Moscow and Peking are both ruled by men who got where they are by brutally conspiring against or eliminating those in their way. (If that sounds stark, read all about it in that candid memoir, *Khrushchev Remembers*. Or better, try to interview Messrs. Malenkov, Molotov, P'eng Teh-huai, or Chen Po-ta.) Conversely, if you happen to believe that Marxist-Leninist indoctrination breeds a dangerously astigmatic and suspicious opponent, you will be accused by some of disfavoring peace, détente, and peaceful coexistence. On the other hand, if you believe that the Soviet leadership would sincerely like to make some kind of long-term peace with the United States, the chances are that you won't pay much attention to Soviet political control in Eastern Europe, or to evidence of its wish to dominate the Mediterranean, the Persian (Arabian) Gulf, and the Indian Ocean, as well as acquiring influence in key countries in Sub-Saharan Africa and Latin America.

We surely need better guides than the left-of-center Western intellectuals, scientists, poets, or musicians, whose analytical powers on this life-and-death matter seem chronically limited to assertions that "the Russians are just like us, and all you need to do is go to their meetings and be nice to them and explain that all Americans are not really warmongers, and then peace will break out." And we do have some first-rate experts on Soviet affairs. But there seems to me a special and curious problem in the professional circles where serious analysis *is* done on these matters. The problem arises when the professional Western Kremlinologists (like their counterparts, the Soviet "Americanologists") apply a species of quasi-theological exegesis to ambiguous and obscure texts in rendering their judgments. At their best these experts can appraise Soviet behavior with accuracy and sensitivity. At their worst they take an unvarying hard line and ascribe permanently malevolent motives; and, given their influence on both governments, they can dangerously perpetuate self-fulfilling prophecies about the other side's behavior (or in a few cases improve understanding).

This little group is extraordinarily important for the profound influence they exercise year after year over policy in Washington (and increasingly in Moscow). The President and the Secretary of State do not get their cues about U.S.-Soviet relations from George Wald or Robert Lowell or Sol Hurok. They get them from the experts in and out of government who have studied deeply the history, politics, economics, culture, sociology, literature, and psychology of that small band of men who have made Soviet policy since 1917.

It is the antennae of these experts that wave in the breeze and pick up signals from both overt and implicit Soviet behavior. It is their conclusions that funnel to diplomatic and political leaders in the United States and the West. They typically conceive of their roles as that of the super-realists, commissioned by their expertise to caution the unwary or naïve to beware of the "permanent operating factors" of Bolshevism (they love to turn Marxist phrases against the Marxists), the built-in enmity, the crafty tactical maneuvering to deceive and soften up the gullible, the probability of treachery, and the danger of lowering one's guard.

Particularly when relations are tense, policy is counseled by senior specialists; for a long time that meant Charles Bohlen, Foy Kohler, Jacob Beam, and the late Llewellyn Thompson (George Kennan proved too soft to be used by government in the last decade). Such advice invariably rests on the belief that the Soviets respect only strength and willingness to resist, and take evidence of U.S. eagerness to compromise as a sign of weakness to be exploited. At the same time, that advice helpfully points to Soviet caution and unwillingness to run high risks of confronting the United States in a war, unless it were certain that the United States would back down.

Many Sovietologists have had their pessimistic reading of history and negotiating experiences reinforced by the grim experience, shared by few other Americans, of living and representing the United States for protracted periods of time in Moscow (all those mentioned above were ambassadors there)—an experience almost guaranteed to leave one cynical, embittered, and ineradicably suspicious of the Byzantine machinations of the men in the Kremlin.

I have deliberately painted a stark picture because I think some professional Sovietologists suffer from an occupational hazard of knowing too much. Just as a cop who always deals with criminals can forget how to behave with nice people, so the mind steeped in the lore of Stalinist repression and Communist negotiating strategy is unlikely to feel comfortable with any slow and maturing changes in the process. A genuine aberration in course is likely to be dismissed as a tactical trick, because there *is* a record of scores of false alarms, all known to the Sovietologist. A belief in a durable détente is likely to be warned against, since there *is* a dismal background of Soviet tactical shifts, and of succumbing to irresistible temptations. Left to themselves, the experts would not likely have proposed as drastic reversals of policy that the non-Kremlinologists Nixon and Kissinger conceived and carried out in the first years of the 1970s.

I am by no means saying that expertise always produces advice for us to act hostilely. Most Sovietologists agree with Kennan's famous "X" article of 1947, which prescribed, on the basis of a theory of Communist dynamism, a containment policy designed to generate realistic Soviet perspectives leading in turn to a mellowing of policy and the possibility of genuinely improved relations with the West; and however Dulles distorted the containment notion, Kennan seems to me to have made a correct diagnosis, and we are enjoying some of its truths today. Moreover, some experts have reviewed their positions with genuine candor. One of the U.S. Government's top Soviet specialists (a hard-liner from way back) told me recently that he now sees that the U.S. Government excessively imported the pre-war model of Nazism to explain Stalinism, and that moreover this model was *still* used to explain Soviet policy. Scholars like Marshall Shulman combine that skeptical realism with hard work to improve understanding.

One of the most striking experiences of my life has been to glimpse, as I have several times, into the other side of the mirror—inside the Soviet internal structure within which Russian "Americanologists" do much the same thing for their masters as American Sovietologists do for the American Government and people. There are curious similarities between the growing corps of U.S. specialists in the Soviet Institute of the United States of America, and their professional American counterparts. Each group is steeped in the history of suspicion and animosity of the other side,

THE CRUMBLING CONSENSUS

to a degree far transcending that of the ordinary foreign affairs professional, not to mention the layman. Each has his antennae out to pick up from the masses of material he patiently sifts through even the faintest signal of potential aggression or deception. A background of a thousand years of invasions on the part of the defensive-minded Russian perfectly matches the ineradicable Pearl Harbor trauma of the intelligence-minded American.

Most troubling of all, the American experts share with their Soviet counterparts the environment of generalized suspicion and ingrained hostility within their respective governments. At best this makes those governments intelligently responsive to important interpretative material from the specialists. But at worst it causes the expert to avoid running the risk of being thought naïve or soft (or even treasonable) by those who head his system. This seems to me potentially dangerous on both sides.

First-hand evidence for this conclusion comes from "gaming" exercises I have run involving *both* groups. I found an astonishing and disturbing similarity between the highly theoretical framework of rigid and stereotyped behavior assumed by American specialists simulating Soviet leaders, and by Soviet specialists simulating American leaders. *Both* tend to construct a frame of reference built of blindered ideological preconceptions about "their" government (i.e., the one they were playing in the exercise). Both imputed to "their" side deeply hostile strategic and political goals toward the other, to which pragmatic policy considerations were made subordinate. The result is that American experts playing Russians are often tougher than the real Russians in that particular situation might be. Conversely, Soviet experts playing Americans are tougher and certainly more ideologically consistent than their real-life models in Washington.

Games are, of course, only one kind of empirical evidence of behavior, albeit an intriguing one. Expertise is far better than ignorance, tempered only by the Rand Corporation expert Konrad Kellen's warning about field research: "A Pole can tell you more nonsense about Poland and what goes on there than you can dream up yourself."

Above all, given the open nature of one society and the closed nature of the other, there *is* a monumental asymmetry between the two. God knows, the United States of America has done some things to be ashamed of. And God knows, the United States recently underwent a bitter agony of spirit that far outdid Moscow in criticism of American acts, policies, and even motives. But it is precisely a national orgy of self-criticism such as this, implying a resilience and the freedom to express it wholly lacking in the Soviet Union (or any other society in which dissent is forbidden), that will in the end preserve America's society and form of government.

In an age of political reformation the Soviet regime is still so blindered, so terrified by open criticism, so brainwashed by its own propaganda, and so hopelessly immobile despite its tactical flexibility, that the future by definition must lie in the free society rather than the closed one. The painful self-flagellation in the American press, public, and the Congress which our Soviet friends so gloated over is precisely what will ultimately save us; the dogmatic myth of monopoly of all political and social virtue, despite glaring defects, is what will weaken them. One can only hope that the process will not consume all of us in its flames.

★ ★ ★ ★

It is not easy to excuse some Western liberals who cannot or will not acknowledge the fact that in a bitter historical irony their cherished values of human compassion have always been the first victims of totalitarian rule, whether "socialist" or any other. Their liberal ideals (which I happen to share) traditionally embody social justice and human dignity. But their own confusion of values was close to complete in the 1930s, when they allowed the theology of Communism to obscure the bloody repressions of Stalinist rule. It is equally pitiable in the 1970s, when they permit the signs

THE CRUMBLING CONSENSUS

of altered Soviet behavior to obliterate continued evidence of Soviet internal repression, coercive imperial rule, and world-wide quest for influence. Only the treatment of Soviet Jews seemed to arouse them.

The centrist Establishmentarian understands better than the left the political values at issue between the systems, largely because he does not try to deny the facts of life under totalitarian rule. But as I have argued throughout, his position is also deeply flawed by the weakness of his instinct for what is humane and just in the economic and social sphere. In its preoccupation with strategy, power struggle, and anti-Communism as an ideology, the center has failed to keep the human perspective in paramount place. And as the ideology of the bureaucratic machine, it has also proved to be continuously out of date in its responses to changing world forces.

Thus we are left with a Hobson's choice: either to go with the center and disregard the painful truths about justice and equality the radicals drive us to confront, or to go with the radicals and shut our eyes to the most elementary facts of the real world. We seem forced to choose between the conservative view of unchanged Soviet malevolence and protracted conflict regardless of momentary shifts and thaws; and the radical-liberal view that the Cold War is over and we now live in a world of détente in which deterrence, balance-of-power politics, and perceptions of Soviet hostility are anti-Communist provocations. The requirement that one make a clear choice between these two interpretations strikes me as a perilous trap set for us by those for whom the price of accepting one truth is to disbelieve something else that may also be true.

I myself see the Soviet ruling elite as determined to avoid a nuclear war, desiring a pragmatic trading partnership with the West, caught in the dilemma of wanting to loosen up but not knowing how, and fearing above all to lose control over its empire, its people's minds, and its self-discipline. I know of no more insightful observation than that of veteran Kremlin-watcher Bertram Wolfe, who said that there are two things the Soviets try with all their might and skill to avoid: all-out war and all-out peace. Policy has no intelligent choice except to proceed on the assumption that both interpretations of Soviet behavior are in some measure true.

★ 4 ★

WHERE DID WE GO WRONG?

The American Style

At the heart of America's recent troubles as an actor in the world arena is a deep spiritual and intellectual confusion that is still not properly diagnosed. The confusion is between ideology and national interest. On the one hand lies the ideology of political freedom and private property, the two institutions that define the innate U.S. antipathy to tyranny and to Communism. On the other hand is the operation of national interest, which determines day-to-day strategy and tactics of any state engaged in international relations.

I suspect that Henry Kissinger saw his essential task as helping President Nixon to revive a classical approach to national interest based on geography and other tangible factors, while reducing the part played by ideology. For thus did Metternich and Castlereagh (about whom Kissinger wrote his Ph.D. dissertation) succeed in rescuing Europe from its destabilizing combination of Russian expansion and Napoleonic crusades. The Holy Alliance started with war and repression, and turned eventually into an ideologically neutral policy of balancing power to keep the peace.

Similarly the Eisenhower-Dulles anti-Communist crusades and the Kennedy and Johnson counterrevolutionary campaigns were supplanted by the Nixon-Kissinger program of superpower contacts and reduced involvement elsewhere. This has supplied a good corrective. But like that which it corrected, it in turn overshot the target. The United States inescapably represents an ideology, one that the American people historically cherish. The fundamental dilemma in American foreign policy will not be resolved until the new *Realpolitik* is somehow reunited with the humanistic traditions of Jefferson and Lincoln.

Many of the specific errors and failures in U.S. foreign policy in recent years stemmed from confusion between tactics and values. As a satisfied, and naturally status-quo-favoring power, the United States sought the world-wide goal of "stability." Stability conformed to the fear of escalation to nuclear war, to the interest in uninterrupted profits from overseas private investments, and to the desire to see the recipients of U.S. aid become viable without perpetual crises. In time, after an unsuccessful propaganda crusade, the United States came to favor the same stability in Communist Eastern Europe despite Russian overlordship there. But we sought that stability far too often at the price of democracy or human rights.

Winston Churchill defended his support of a rather gamy régime in Greece in the mid-1940s by saying, "When wolves are about, the shepherd must tend his flock, even if he doesn't much care for mutton." This is a fair slogan in wartime and in terms of real wolves. But somewhat the same argument was being made three decades later to justify aid to and close relations with an equally gamy Greek government that despite shuffled leaders had junked the Constitution and substituted a modified police state. In both hot and cold wars, a pragmatic policy of collaboration with tyranny becomes hypocrisy if one pretends to be acting in the name of political freedom. (The bankruptcy of such a policy was complete when Greece, along with Spain and Turkey, refused

WHERE DID WE GO WRONG?

the United States the use of their lands to resupply Israel in the 1973 war, despite the fact that the almost $10 billion in U.S. aid had been increasingly defended on grounds of Mid-East policy.)

The underlying justification for U.S. support of Greece in both the 1940s and 1970s was the strategic competition with the Soviet Union. But a wartime exaggeration by which not only Greece but also Russia (and China) became honorary democracies was no longer supportable in a period in which such competition as remained was political, economic, social, and, perhaps above all, psychological. What remained of the Cold War in the mid-1970s was a contest that turned not simply on readiness to honor military commitments, but on whether the forms of political and social philosophy advocated are authentic or merely snake oil.

If this is the most important factor in the recent distress with U.S. foreign policy, it was also the least acknowledged by policymakers. In almost every instance where Washington appeared to be propping up and even bedding down with undemocratic tyrants, inside the U.S. Government a case had been made which, whatever else one may have thought of it, had sufficient logic to win the day. This logic was rarely if ever shared with the American people.

Thus one can and should acknowledge that after the "Colonel's Coup" in Greece in 1967, the United States was the *only* Western nation to take tangible steps of disapproval. But the June 1967 Middle East war subordinated that distaste to the need for ready access to support Israel. In the case of Pakistan's savage repression of self-determination in East Pakistan in 1971, the simultaneously-occurring Nixon-Kissinger turnabout on China policy required a secure, secret, and reliable route of communication, and this won out over a policy of pressure based on moral considerations. Continued U.S. support for South Vietnamese President Thieu, even after he had made a farce of recent Presidential elections, was apparently weighed against the criticism that would come if the United States treated him like a full-fledged puppet and, like Moscow (and Washington in 1961), simply intervened and replaced him.

None of these arguments in favor of supporting malodorous régimes persuades me; but at least the decisions were not whimsical. If the argument could have been made that we were averting a massive upset in the all-important relative equilibrium of world forces (which it could not), I might have been converted. What turned these "pragmatic" examples of *Realpolitik*, engaged in by many a government, into an American tragedy was the chronic refusal of the U.S. Government to tell people the truth, to curtail the hypocritical rhetoric, or to weigh sufficiently in the balance the humane and moral factor in our relations with the world outside of superpower relations where other values are at stake.

It is hard to think of a more fateful early turning point for U.S. foreign policy than 1956, when the Government decided that it could not tolerate a Vietminh victory in the promised elections to be held in South Vietnam. In other words, the United States would not accept the results even if won in a free election. In one swoop the United States repudiated the 1954 Geneva Agreement on Vietnam, betrayed the fundamental ideal of democracy—to trust the people to decide their political fate in free elections—and ensured that in the future, since a Vietnamese solution was ruled out by Washington, there would have to be an American solution.

Even then explanations were privately circulated that Ho Chi Minh was bound to win such an election and that the ensuing communization of South Vietnam would present unacceptable security threats to the United States—threats that were never spelled out except in erroneous terms of Moscow or Peking domination of Vietnam, which we have learned is not the way things are at all. One can concede that President Eisenhower and his advisers sincerely believed that U.S. security could not afford the results of a democratic process. But there and in all the other instances I have cited of a belief that a worse evil would be avoided by supporting undemocratic régimes, the Government, instead of explaining, invariably propagandized and finally outraged the American people.

Official rhetoric undermined its own credibility every time it persisted in speaking of "preserving freedom" where freedom was being suppressed, even alluding to our own "revolutionary" nature. The gulf between rhetoric and actuality thus widened, and policy often became a distorted parody of something that once had great meaning. The style with which such problems were dealt with more and more bore out Charles de Gaulle's aphorism that "The United States brings to great affairs elementary feelings and a complicated policy" (*Call to Honor* [New York: Viking Press, 1955], Vol. I, p. 209). The tragic result was that, while using the words of democracy, we ourselves seemed to lose its very core, and the costs to this nation began to surpass the sought-for benefits as millions of Americans, old and young, turned away in disgust from the indifference to human values and the hypocrisy with which it was defended.

Mixing simplified ideology with hard-nosed pragmatism and presenting the mix as idealistic was supposed to provide tactical freedom of action to achieve the noble strategic end of preserving democracy. But it often brought instead the worst of both worlds. In the name of democratic ends we would (like our Soviet adversary) often subject third countries to such undemocratic means as clandestine subversion or support of local tyranny. And the more we did that, the more the U.S. Government found it necessary to subject the American people to evasion, and itself to self-deception.

It was not too long ago that American leaders acted as though the nation's most precious historic asset was its reputation for espousing political freedom and civil rights, however unpopular it made us with tyrants. But in mobilizing a crusade against the Communist version of totalitarian dictatorial rule, the U.S. Government often seemed willing to embrace virtually any other totalitarians *so long as they were not Communists*. We engaged our fortunes with unpopular and sometimes tyrannical régimes in the name of both anti-Communism and stability. But, in the end, anti-Communism was a weak ideology, in large part because we were not in fact always found supporting freedom. And stability was a poor goal because the price of always favoring short-term stability at whatever cost is to generate uncontrollable revolutionary tides. John F. Kennedy was at his wisest when he said, "Those who make peaceful revolution impossible will make violent revolution inevitable" (March 13, 1962).

In an historical period in which the problem is *not* at root a defense against military aggression, such a policy was not only wrong, but dubious by even the most pragmatic standards. Let me quote just one observer with regard to just one country—Spain. Speaking of the inevitable struggle for power in that strategically important Atlantic-Mediterranean promontory, C. L. Sulzberger soberly wrote from Madrid:

> The sad thing is that the United States, in advance of this inevitable struggle, is seen by a powerful group of forces including the youth, the universities, the liberals, the intellectuals and large segments of the church and business as a right-wing influence committed to supporting the most reactionary solution. ("Lining Up Against the Future," *New York Times*, December 27, 1970)

He went on to remark, "This is especially tragic because it surely cannot be the intended U.S. position." And the sad truth is that this applies to a score of other once admiring countries as well. Greece is another unfortunately obvious example. A first-class American journalist wrote from Athens in the summer of 1973:

> Virtually all Greeks, from the Macedonian peasant to the sophisticated Athenian businessman, believe that the U.S. supports the colonel's regime 100 percent. Most are equally convinced that the U.S. put the regime in power. Greeks universally believe that the U.S. supports the dictatorship in exchange for the considerable military advantages it enjoys in Greece. (John K. Cooley in the *Christian Science Monitor*, July 26, 1973)

Contrary to the assertions of some critics, U.S. military alliances and arrangements have not been all or even mostly like that, but in fact have primarily been with democratically-elected governments of the West. But even within the NATO family—our premier military alliance—Portugal permits only a few more civil liberties to its citizens than Russia, China, Cuba, or North Vietnam. Turkey is under indirect military rule, and Spain as honorary anchorman of NATO is still basically run by the Falangist régime overwhelmingly condemned by the United Nations in 1946.

The Organization of American States covers all of Latin America except Cuba, which on U.S. initiative in 1962 was excluded from participation because of its association with the Communist powers. But up to ten of the other members of the OAS deny to their people elementary rights of political expression, not to mention economic and social opportunity. According to a former American ambassador to Costa Rica, Secretary Dulles informed him, before his departure to take up his duties, that "The dictators are the Chiefs of State on whom we must depend in Latin America."

Among the major beneficiaries of U.S. commitments and support, and on U.S. insistence made one of the five permanent members of the original U.N. Security Council, the Nationalist Chinese Government never consulted its great majority of thirteen million native Taiwanese as to whether they wanted to live under Chiang Kai Shek's rule (or for that matter, Mao Tse Tung's). Our "tilt" toward Pakistan cost the American reputation dearly in the December 1971 India-Pakistan war, since it was at the time ruled by a not very intelligent military dictator engaged in a genocidal slaughter of political and ethnic opponents in East Pakistan at least as ruthless as when the Hitlerites and Stalinists disposed of their undesirables. Our Philippine ally has become a virtual dictatorship. In Africa the principal recipients of U.S. aid—Ethiopia and Liberia—are as dictatorial and undemocratic as, say, Hanoi, and no one I know can remember the last time free elections were held in Iran, Laos, or Cambodia. Many *can* remember the last free election in South Vietnam, an election giving a one-man choice to a people for whose "right to choose freely their own future" fifty-five thousand Americans died. Thailand—the remaining bastion of U.S. strategy in Asia—was a military dictatorship until 1973. And so it goes.

Such extreme "pragmatism" might be justifiable if the U.S. were truly at war or if those countries were being directly threatened by an external invader (whether self-styled "national liberation" or not) aiming at dominating a continent or region to the detriment of every other nation's security, including our own. In some instances this has been true. But even where it was not, U.S. support of client states was invariably put in terms of advancing the practice of democracy and the enjoyment of political freedom. If liberals in power disguise their causes (e.g., foreign aid) as interests, the practitioners of *Realpolitik* with equal lack of candor dress up their interests as causes.

A few years ago it was fashionable to decry the American tendency to blend idealism with legalism, and in the process to short-change the needful pragmatism. George Kennan and Hans Morgenthau made this point twenty years ago in their splendid books respectively entitled *American Diplomacy* and *In Defense of the National Interest*. My impression is that the idealism continued to define the nation's purposes, while the means used became increasingly expedient. If that makes us sound like the Communists, it is meant to. That growing disjunction of ends and means, locked in place in a mammoth civil-military bureaucratic machine, seems to me a far more plausible explanation of our recent troubles than the Marxist diagnosis of calculated economic greed and conscious imperialistic ambition.

With the Vietnam War the confusion between the nation's purposes and practices reached its grand climax. Indeed, if U.S. intervention in Vietnam had been the calculated act of imperialist ambition charged by the left, it would have been in many ways easier to fight, and surely to understand—if not to condone. Instead, in one of history's ironies, Vietnam represented a combination of doctrinaire anti-Communism plus the political idealism that stems from Wilsonian self-determination and U.N. Charter strictures against aggression. As the intervention wore on, the United States came to enjoy the worst of both pragmatism and idealism.

Traditionally priding itself on its pragmatism and avoidance of the rigidities of doctrine, the U.S. Government discouraged long-range planning, ridiculed theorizing, and avoided philosophy. Instead, the questions were posed pragmatically and incrementally: "Do we or don't we up the ante by 20,000 (or 200,000, or 600,000)?" "What do we tell Westmoreland when McNamara/Taylor/Rostow goes out there next week?" "How much can we get away with without having to go to the Congress?" "How will the election year affect our ability to increase the force levels?" And so forth. This was pragmatism with a vengeance.

At the same time, however, doctrinal anti-Communism that would not distinguish between Russia, China, and Vietnam so dominated the minds of those in charge that from Eisenhower to Johnson they were unable to disengage, or even to consider changes in policy dictated by the fact that, as has been amply shown in the writings of former officials, *no one* in government was prepared to demonstrate that there was a good chance of any of the contemplated policies' succeeding in a reasonable future. If the Soviets balance their books every night in the sense of knowing when to liquidate an unsuccessful commitment, the United States most assuredly does not.

That is not conscious imperialism; it is rather a form of high-level incompetence. But with it an *unconsciously* imperialist mentality had crept into the American outlook during the period, and we are only now beginning to shake it off. It took hold in the postwar years as the policy arrangements to counter Soviet thrusts solidified by the mid-1950s, and it persisted in official and "Establishment" thinking thereafter. It took the form of an unstated belief that American omnipotence carried with it a kind of omniscience. Its error was to regard U.S. leadership—indispensable when other free nations were flat on their backs—as permanent and inherent. This was plausible in a world in which for a while the United States was the universal makeweight, and in which U.S. action or inaction would decisively influence the outcome of virtually all quarrels, conflicts, and problems. But, in addition —let's face it—it embodied a frank taste for power. So, by the time it was appropriate to begin to modulate and alter the posture, the strategy was set in concrete, and a whole generation trained to operate it was in power.

Partly this is the great time lag in the process of democracy's reorienting itself to a new situation—as the American people did in the period 1941-45. We can now see that by the mid-1950s, when the post-war institutions of containment and Cold War had been developed—NATO, SEATO, the Baghdad Pact, the 1947 National Security Council machinery, vast military budgets, and all the rest—they were beginning even then to be unresponsive to still newer developments in fissioning alliances, multipolarity, mutual deterrence, and the revival of economic, social, and cultural forces that had been suppressed by the war and the fear of a new holocaust.

But it was fantastically hard to adapt. The compass was locked on course and the engines were turning full blast. Secretary Dulles was chasing off after military allies around the world. China was written off as a Soviet stooge long after evidence began to flow in of breaks in Sino-Soviet solidarity; Hanoi and Pyonyang were labeled Chinese puppets despite the centuries of conflict between them and China; and the protracted conflict between Soviet Communism and American capitalism was still seen as primarily military rather than what the Soviet leaders themselves announced it to be. Despite the ineffable facts of mutual strategic deterrence, there was escalation in the strategic arms build-ups, accompanied by qualitatively destabilizing changes such as the Anti-Ballistic Missile (ABM) and MIRV multiple warheads, the one checked with the first SALT agreement of 1972, the other not at all.

One of the results of engaging in power politics but calling it idealism was the tendency to reject information when it did not conform to one's preconceptions—another little habit better left to the Politburos of this world. In the Vietnam War at least a couple of Presidents and their topmost advisers simply refused to accept the evidence of their eyes, their common sense, or their expensive intelligence services. The resulting inflexibility of mind also created missed opportunities and even had the inadvertent effect of encouraging such Soviet victories as the leapfrog into the Middle East over Mr. Dulles's "northern tier" of military alliances. I myself finally left the State Department because of the latter example of Mr. Dulles's neo-theological approach to foreign relations.

During 1956 I was the Department's policy planner for U.N. affairs. As such I was intensively engaged, in co-operation with members of the Policy Planning Staff, in trying to maintain a longer-range component in the mounting crisis over the Egyptian takeover of the Suez Canal. The Dulles preference for vest-pocket diplomacy combined with British and French pigheadedness and Israeli frustration to bring on a savage little war. After the Suez fiasco of early November 1956 there seemed, for the first time since 1948, a magic moment of opportunity to come to grips with the central substantive issues of the Arab-Israeli conflict—i.e., borders, Palestine refugees, and waterways. In those wild midnight sessions of the U.N. Special Emergency General Assembly, whipsawed by the simultaneously exploding Hungarian crisis, a couple of resolutions were even drafted and introduced into the United Nations to deal with those gut issues for the first time in a decade of unremitting conflict between Arabs and Israel.

My colleagues and I labored to devise some proposals building on these possibilities. Secretary Dulles had meanwhile disappeared to his retreat on Duck Island in Canada. He returned clutching a paper embodying his solution to the Middle East nightmare. It became the Eisenhower Doctrine—a plan for the equivalent of a military alliance stretching from the Mediterranean across the Middle East, under whose terms any state threatened by military aggression backed by "international communism" would be helped upon request by the United States. In short, the problem as he saw it was Russian military invasion of the Middle East, and he had little or no interest in the central issues that had set the area aflame. So much for policy planning —or even rational diplomacy. (In fairness it must be said that Dulles, like Eden, was a sick man during the crisis.)

As the Dulles plan began to be discussed, the American ambassador in Moscow sent frantic cables explaining in every way open to his vocabulary that, of all things that might happen in the Middle East, and of all the plans the Soviet leaders might harbor, the least likely contingency was a Soviet-sponsored invasion of the Middle East. When shortly afterward M.I.T. offered the chance to direct a new study of the future of the United Nations and its relation to U.S. national interests, I took my leave.

★ ★ ★ ★

The growing quarrel at home over U.S. foreign policy can be explained at least in part by the clash between two idealisms. One was the "naïve" idealism of the young, who, while often ignorant of the historical realities, saw perhaps more clearly than anyone else that the Emperor, despite his noble rhetorical garments, had become a naked Bismarck who wouldn't admit it. Opposed to this was the "sophisticated" idealism of their officials and other elders who believed that the nobility of American purpose was self-explanatory, and thus transcended the dirty pool they felt they had to play to "win" the game. At worst, this brought a corrupting loss of human perspectives in whose absence strategy is without redeeming morality.

I was recently visited by a South Vietnamese leader who served in the cabinets of both Diem and Thieu, but is now a university dean. He obviously considered President Thieu an American puppet with little other support. His voice shook as he told me how America's failure to "permit" free choice to South Vietnam in 1971 lost us what little respect remained in his country, particularly among the youth, for the vaunted American purpose of "self-determination" for the Vietnamese people. Perhaps his emotion sprang from humiliation at Vietnamese impotence in the face of Washington's dictation as to who would and would not rule his country; or perhaps it was frustration at our shortsightedness in once again setting temporary "stability" above the values for which we claimed to have sent our youth to die. He recently told an all-Asian conference of non-Communist leaders that "liberalism and Marxism have been the two ideologies in whose names Americans, Russians, Chinese and others have turned many countries, Vietnam in particular, into a vale of tears."

The spiritual confusion under discussion was nicely caught by Max Frankel, Washington correspondent of the *New York Times*, in his parody of Chairman Mao's imagined reactions to the 1972 Nixon China visit, in which he had "Mao" speak of the ambiguity of the American ideology:

> How could I ever mistake these Americans for the No. 1 enemy? It is their opportunism that misleads. They do whatever is convenient or necessary, but with such ideological passion that they frighten everyone into thinking them irrational. (*New York Times*, March 5, 1972)

Misplaced idealism, spiritual confusion, arrogance, pride—these are besetting sins enough. But in addition, we have been poor students of history, bad listeners, chronically ignorant of foreign cultures (how many Americans can speak even one foreign language decently?), bemused with gadgetry, and frequently obsessed with physical and material power. Not all Americans. Just too many of those chosen from Middle and Upper America and its suburbs who have helped run the post-war policy machine.

I have in mind some State Department and White House

civilian officials playing the part of General Buck Turgidson in *Dr. Strangelove* instead of that of the diplomat whose sacred duty is to avert violence and find compromise ways to peace. I think of my Cambridge friends as Special Assistants to Presidents, acting like the grand viziers of the Sultan—haughty, infected with power, suddenly incapable of the humanistic reasoning that previously distinguished them. I think of a U.S. military attaché in Guatemala who assured me in 1967 that the only hope was the re-election of the dictator currently ruling that benighted place.

This brings me to a final point, which should pain us more than perhaps any other. If there was any final, fallback American quality in which we could justly take pride, it was our "know-how." Even if one studied nothing about a foreign land, spoke no foreign language, and knew none of the queer foreign customs, after all, people were people, weren't they? And they all want schoolhouses, better crop yields, healthier children, contested elections, secret ballots, more efficient police forces, and straighter roads, don't they?

But it turned out in country after country of the Third World that what we could do at home was not necessarily exportable; that people were resistant to having their affairs arranged for them; and that we were not all that good at telling them how to organize their community life, conduct their politics, or educate their young. I am not speaking here of the worst of our overseas presence—the blundering American, the exploiting company, the blind militarist. I am speaking of some of our *best*. There were obvious exceptions, such as the brilliant (non-governmental) success in introducing miracle wheat and rice strains, not to mention countless individual cases of successful U.S. advice and technical assistance. But the record is equally full of instances of aid pumped into the hands of elites who continued to resist land reform and dodge taxes, of machinery rusting in disuse after the technical assistance mission left, of "self-defense" hardware and manpower turned on a neighboring country. There is probably still a good deal we could do for some people; moreover, we were a much nicer breed when we tried to help others instead of putting it all in cost/benefit terms. But the picture of the American idealist confidently striding into a distant tropical town armed with universally applicable know-how including steel-tipped plow, intra-uterine loops, and homilies on democracy is, with a few exceptions, a neo-Kiplingesque relic.

The Military Bias

One of the most undesirable changes in America has been the vast increase in the role of the military in recent years. It cannot, however, be analyzed on a basis of the myth, perpetrated by the Left and parroted by some liberals, that the Pentagon "runs the country." The inescapable fact is that we the people, through our elected representatives, voted the enormous defense budgets, legislated the weapons systems programs and mutual assistance treaties, and created the draft, not to mention the Tonkin Gulf Resolution and other guidelines for a military cast to policy. Under our system, soldiers do what their civilian leaders tell them to do. It is to the credit of the American military establishment that, despite widespread discontent among many of its best professionals because of foreign policies that in their view misused the military (notably in Vietnam), they generally still respect that tradition.

Moreover, after World War II the problem *was*, to a frightening degree, a military one, when the United States demobilized as though there would be no tomorrow while the Soviet Union not only kept several million men under arms but also maintained its troops in East Germany, Poland, Hungary, and Rumania in order to enforce the communization of Eastern Europe. There is no need to reopen all the arguments about that question here, except to note that while Moscow's desire to ensure secure Western borders was understandable, only a very careless historian can wipe out the asymmetry between Western plans for relaxation and the renewed Soviet thrust for political power, or the succession of crises touched off by the Berlin Blockade in 1948 and the North Korean attack on South Korea in 1950.

The revisionists cheat most of all in playing down the fact that it was only *after* the North Korean aggression that the United States finally mobilized its military and industrial strength and embarked on the mammoth build-up. They are strangely silent about the fact that U.S. defense budgets were in the neighborhood of $15 billion or so in the pre-1950 era of Defense Secretary Louis Johnson (during which time military men, far from influencing foreign policy, were actually forbidden to consort with the State department). It was during the same period that the famous National Security Council paper "NSC 68" was drafted, calling for an enormous regearing of the United States to finance and confront the torrent of challenges and hostility that had issued from Moscow since Stalin's famous February 1946 speech calling for renewed vigilance and hostility plus reinforcement of Soviet armed might.

Even then, NSC 68 had no tangible results until *after* the Korean War began; then the enormous American response vastly outdistanced what the planners under Policy Planning Staff director Paul Nitze had recommended. The revisionist argument rests on the fact that the United States had the atomic bomb in 1945 and that some Americans wanted to use it to pressure the Russians (who got their bomb in 1949). I can only say that objectively it had precious little effect in stopping the takeover of Eastern Europe, the Berlin Blockade, or the Korean attack, even if the United States *had* tried to brandish it menacingly—which it did not. Instead, the United States offered to turn the whole thing over to the United Nations under a world-wide system of control in which the United States would have no veto. Some blackmailers!

I have been arguing that by the late 1950s and early 1960s the

WHERE DID WE GO WRONG?

problem had begun to alter in important ways. But let it not be forgotten that there were also continuing challenges of the old sort. Perhaps the most notable was Soviet Premier Khrushchev's implied threat to go to war if the United States did not knuckle under to his version of a German Peace Treaty with a Berlin "solution" eliminating all Western rights. His first ultimatum was set off in 1958 with a six-month fuse, and was renewed for several extension periods. This singularly nasty episode culminated in the Berlin crisis of 1961, which could not have been more military, what with tanks drawn up muzzle to muzzle, and the Russians erecting overnight their obscene wall to pen in the remaining East Germans, since the flow to the West had by then reached hemorrhage proportions. (I am here expressing the almost physical revulsion I experienced in first seeing and traversing the Wall; I must admit that it became an element in stabilizing the volatile Berlin situation and preventing new, potentially nuclear crises.) Nor could the Cuban missile crisis of 1962 have been more military, although we can all be grateful that it was resolved with diplomacy rather than in the traditional way.

One price of mounting a vast peacetime military build-up was to empower military men in ways they had before enjoyed only in wartime. To some extent, military advice was crucial to the kinds of responses the United States felt it could and could not make to various challenges of the earlier post-war period. But in the end, the Defense Department became so monstrously big that whether it actually wants to or not, it *does* exercise power over much of U.S. industry and industry's political representatives, in addition to millions of civilian and uniformed personnel. Yet to my mind, the highest cost for this nation arose when military power and force began to be the dominant theme in much of U.S. foreign policy. That happened not because the generals took over, but because civilian leadership gave excessive weight to the military factor. For far too long, European policy was a NATO operation, revolution was a "threat" to be physically opposed, insurgency a technical military problem, and crisis something one dealt with through the NSC political-military machinery invented for the world of 1947.

It is this last development that I want to discuss, for it gravely compounded our problems. As I argued earlier, the paramount error in post-war U.S. foreign policy was to apply indiscriminately to Third World situations the reasoning that went into the earlier political-military confrontation with the Soviet Union in Europe and in Korea. But—and this is the point here—it was not only the military who reacted in stereotyped ways. It was also their civilian masters who increasingly thought in military terms and consequently gave disproportionate weight to military factors and advice. In the process they seriously abdicated their responsibilities as civilians, as diplomats, and as peacemakers. The respected strategic analyst Bernard Brodie described very well the "crux of the matter—the militarization of the thinking of the American political leadership as a result of the shibboleths of the Cold War and of the new-found eminence of the United States as 'leader of the free world' " (in a book review in *Survival*, January 1971, p. 33).

The worst sin committed within the U.S. Government was not that the military did what we trained and paid them to do—including taking a deliberately limited view that spares us from having a bunch of philosophers debating fine metaphysical points when from time to time we tell them to go somewhere for us and run the risk of being killed.

No, the worst sin is that so many Presidents and Secretaries and Under Secretaries of State and Special Assistants to the President have been seduced by the lure of donning the Field Marshal's uniform; or—what is just as bad—have tried to re-enact the Company Commander or the PT officer or the Deputy Chief of Staff they had once been; or, worse still, have failed to assert the civil primacy enjoined by both our Constitution and common sense, instead deferring to or emulating the far narrower judgments of military advisers on matters with important political, economic, social, psychological, and cultural aspects.

My own impression was that some of our civilian leaders and advisers quite forgot what it was they were supposed to do. The State Department "role" (or that of the White House when it usurps that role) is surely to speak up for the classic diplomatic and political purposes of minimizing and preventing conflict, seeking compromise, utilizing time-stretching devices, popular debate, and judgment, and thinking twice before intervening, all of which also makes for caution and lack of boldness—failings for which many of us have admittedly criticized State.

During the late 1960s I was invited to Washington (reportedly because no insider could be chosen without offending another insider) to act as chairman of the "U.S." group in a high-level planning exercise pretesting some extremely vital decisions concerning future strategic weapons systems. In "my" group were several top-ranking military men, including both the then Chief of Staff of the U.S. Army and the Commanding General of the North American Air Defense Command (NORAD). But the most militaristic, unpolitical, and recklessly escalatory of all was a top official of the State Department. His defense (for he has a reputation as an intelligent man) would doubtless be that it was only an exercise. I just don't believe that. You do not deliberately look like a fool in front of your peers in Washington. But—unfortunately—you *do* try to look, sound, and act "tough-minded." And in the post-war Government this meant a perverse willingness to see military solutions as invariably relevant. This distortion seems to have become ingrained in the top civilian mentality in the U.S. governmental and diplomatic establishment by the time we were rescued from it by the mounting revulsion of the American people at the unending Vietnam War. In this connection Psychologist Irving Janis in a mind-stretching book about consensus pressures entitled *Victims of Groupthink* (Boston: Houghton Mifflin, 1967) explains the 1961 Bay of Pigs fiasco in part by the "virile poses" conveyed in the rhetoric used by representatives of the CIA and the Joint Chiefs of Staff. He analyzes the responses of State Department representatives as "becoming anxious to show that they were not softheaded idealists but were really just as tough as the military men" (page 41).

It helped that President Nixon was not so much intimidated or impressed by generals as Lyndon Johnson (or Harry Truman). Henry Kissinger was expert in facing down military figures who were accustomed to insisting on a particular strategy or arms level or budget item as "vital to the security of the nation." Perhaps it takes someone with the arrogance of a Harvard or M.I.T. professor to believe his geopolitical, strategic, and even tactical judgments to be as good as or better than those of a four-star admiral. In the 1970s this produced some shifts toward more traditional forms.

But even Mr. Nixon as President occasionally reflected the post-war distortion of roles. In a January 1972 announcement to White House reporters of a further troop reduction in Vietnam, Nixon stated that the action had the "approval" of Secretary of Defense Laird and Admiral Thomas H. Moorer, Chairman of the Joint Chiefs of Staff (*International Herald Tribune,* January 14, 1972)—two people whom he had appointed, and whose "approval" could be only for public relations, not Constitutional, reasons.

One of the elements in standard military thinking that is most destructive when imported into political decision-making is the tendency to make "worst case" analysis. Adam Yarmolinsky, who served as both Deputy Assistant Secretary of Defense and Assistant to Secretary McNamara, is worth quoting on the subject of this tendency:

> A second [military] habit is to emphasize readiness for the worst contingency that might arise, a rule best illustrated by American policy in Europe, in which priority consistently went to preparedness for a massive assault mounted in secrecy and launched suddenly and surprisingly by the Soviets. It was much more difficult, as a result, to test whether the U.S.S.R. might be willing to settle some European issues. Between 1950 and 1953, the Truman Administration rejected all Soviet suggestions for negotiations on an all-German peace treaty. In 1957–1958 the Eisenhower Admin-

istration rejected Polish Foreign Minister Adam Rapacki's scheme for making Central Europe a denuclearized zone. On both occasions, as cautious and hard-eyed Western analysts now read the evidence, the Soviets may have had a genuine desire for some kind of agreement. The United States did not follow up Soviet overtures in large part because if agreements were reached, it believed NATO would be less able to lay preparations for the worst contingency.

He makes the same criticism of U.S. Vietnam policy:

> American thinking was concentrated here, too, on a "worst contingency"—a full-scale North Korean, Chinese or North Vietnamese invasion—and such thinking precluded the diplomacy of looking toward a longer run. (*The Military Establishment—Its Impacts on American Society* [New York: Harper and Row, 1971], pp. 146–47)

A related problem was the tendency of the military to preface virtually all planning and action studies with something entitled "Definition of the Threat." Now, while for military purposes this is often appropriate, there are four things wrong with it. First, it makes all policies reactive to what someone else is doing or thinking about doing. Second, like the outlook of the policeman in a tough neighborhood, it regards everything as a menace rather than as an opportunity or even just a problem, and it does this chiefly by looking at *capabilities* rather than *intentions*. Third, when it is borrowed by civilian planners to preface their thinking, it destroys the power of creative initiative by keeping policy locked onto a military agenda in which problems are defined in terms of other nations' military capabilities.

The fourth thing wrong with it was articulated by Dean Acheson, who was never intimidated by anyone, even generals:

> I have long noticed that military recommendations are usually premised upon the meticulous statement of assumptions that as often as not are quite contrary to the facts and yet control the conclusions. (*Present at the Creation* [New York: Norton, 1969], p. 451)

His example—a devastating one for which he must share responsibility—was the near-fatal U.S./U.N. march north to the Yalu after driving the invaders out of South Korea in the fall of 1950.

This combination of "worst case" planning and "threat assessment" seemed to me gravely to reduce the capacity of civilian (and even military) leaders to see issues clearly. Instead, it chronically hindered them from getting ahead of their problems sufficiently to avoid having to react blindly to someone else's capabilities. A pair of legitimate technical methods for military staff planning thus distorted the very nature of American decision-making on broad policy.

It would not have been so disastrous if on the civilian side there were accepted techniques of planning and analysis on the same range of problems, methods that competed fairly with those of the military. But there were few if any such techniques, and where they existed in the research community they were dismissed by senior political and diplomatic officials as "theoretical" —which many of course were. Perhaps because of this allergy the civilian policy official tends to commit a sin almost precisely the reverse of the military error—that of making "best case" estimates. Because there is no ingrained or accepted analytical method of foreign policy analysis that commands the respect of those placed in high position, the options finally chosen often represent simply the political leader's hunch as to what will work. Sometimes it is not even that, but what he imagines he has to do within "realistic" political limits.

John F. Kennedy, on the testimony of all his lieutenants, felt uneasy about the wisdom and the chances of success of the CIA-planned invasion of Cuba by an army of émigrés, but rode along with the military judgments (and overrode the misgivings of some of his civilian advisers) until the eventual 1961 disaster of the Bay of Pigs. His reaction was reported to be that he would never listen to the experts again. But that seems to me equally wrong. For in the case of Vietnam it was the CIA intelligence analysts and the State Department's Bureau of Intelligence and Research who accurately reported the facts and the prospects as they saw them in Vietnam. It was a politician-President, fed by zealous subordinates, who fixed obsessively on one course of action and rejected as virtually treasonable all competing judgments, while his Secretary of State reportedly dismissed some proposals to explore basic alternate strategies as "speculative"—presumably meaning unworthy of attention.

In some desperation (as well as scholarly interest) Cornelius Gearin and I in a 1968 "political game" designed a mock structure for building into U.S. diplomatic decision-making some elements of a more formal cost/benefit analysis, plus *"worst*-case" outcomes to correct for euphoric U.S. political hunch-playing in response to crisis situations. When our game "President" and his "advisers" chewed over the potential intervention situation we had given them and then began to close on a preferred course of action (typically a minimal investment of funds and perhaps a few military training advisers), we had a former Federal budget official march into their crisis-management "NSC" meeting and proceed to put up charts showing alternative outcomes and raising questions that we were not certain were always asked. (*What if things go wrong and you have to increase the commitment, and you're still there five years from now—like, shall we say, in Vietnam?*)

In addition, our "Budget Director" served up costs of the decisions: not only financial costs, or best-case costs (with the United States in and out in six months), but what the economists call "opportunity costs" of the worst outcomes, i.e., cities not cleaned up, schools not built, inflationary spirals, and the like. A splendid soldier and civic leader, General James R. Gavin, U.S.A. Ret., who was my "President" in that exercise, told me later that afterward he recommended to Washington that this kind of process be built into the White House Situation Room. I do not know whether it ever was.

On treating crisis situations in the Third World as though they were primarily military and political rather than a whole range of other things as well, one of America's finest—and worst treated—senior diplomats, former Ambassador to the U.N. Charles W. Yost, has written, on the basis of his first-hand knowledge:

> One consequence, in view of the composition and unconscious bias of the Council [National Security Council], has been all too often to accord undue weight to military factors in assessing foreign policy problems. The seemingly neutral meshing of foreign policy decision-making into the NSC machinery over the past decade has therefore in fact further warped that decision-making in a military direction and is to a substantial degree responsible for some of the most serious misjudgments of that period. ("The Instruments of U.S. Foreign Policy," *Foreign Affairs*, October 1971, p. 64)

Excessive emphasis on military factors in foreign policy has led to a final distortion—namely, treating military power as an end in itself, rather than a means to other ends, to be used only as a desperate last resort and representing an admission of complete diplomatic failure. It is in turn part of a mindless larger tendency to treat all power as an end in itself, such as the drive to be the most powerful of all ("Number One").

Some may believe it immoral to treat military power as a *means* to a political end. It is sad but true that this turns out to be the only rational approach in a planet still armed to the teeth, and with no world government in sight. Franklin D. Roosevelt's wartime policy of "unconditional surrender," combined with his indignant dismissal of Churchill's worries about what Europe would look like after the fighting, plus Eisenhower's apolitical decision to permit the victors in the West to be isolated in Berlin a hundred miles from Western territory—these contributed to the Cold War every bit as much as the Soviet use of military power to achieve national and ideological ends in the same war.

Roosevelt's costly policy of refusing to allow "dirty" political considerations to sully "pure" military ends represents one of America's most pernicious traditions. By deferring all "political" questions until after "victory," such a policy contributed toward ensuring that the United States would not benefit from a more stable world. Communist leaders such as Stalin and Mao never made this error, perhaps because, unlike American politicians, they studied theory—in this case the theories of Karl von Clausewitz.

The blind impetus that military power seems to follow once such power is acquired—the need to improve it, replace it, even exercise it like a horse—has contributed on both sides to what former Defense Secretary Robert McNamara once called the "mad momentum" of the nuclear arms race. Former Pentagon weapons chief Herbert York soberingly chronicled the effect of this dynamic element in decisions in the 1950s and 1960s to build new and costlier strategic and tactical weapons systems that could not in fact serve any rational need. (See *Race to Oblivion*, New York: Simon and Schuster, 1970.) Like expanding industrial and commercial conglomerates, military establishments given sufficient means can become protean and insatiable, requiring vast amounts of feeding just to stay in place, let alone stay modern.

In the longer term we'd better see to it that we have a strong-minded President, an arrogant Cambridge professor at his side, and an unshakeably critical Senate Foreign Relations Committee Chairman, if the Republic is to be spared new involvements arising from the need of the military establishment to get some exercise.

And Then the Lying

The deepest symptom of political disorder in the United States of late has been the growing belief that its leaders lie to the people. In election politics honesty was always a rarity, and the

Watergate cover-up escalated a habit to a crime. In foreign policy the people's trust has also been tampered with.

On February 8, 1971, when South Vietnamese troops were sent into Laos, NBC television news reported that 46 per cent of the thousand Americans polled at random throughout the country believed that *despite President Nixon's denial* the United States in fact had ground troops in Laos. (Apparently the United States did not, apart from the fairly well-known CIA operation in support of the Meo tribesmen, and technically these were not ground troops). Three months later more than two-thirds of the Americans of voting age in a Gallup poll sample of 1,599 stated their belief that the Nixon Administration was failing to tell the American people all they should know about the conduct of the Vietnam War; only 21 per cent believed that the public was being leveled with. In late 1972 the figures were almost identical (and in 1973 approximately the same majority believed that the President possessed guilty knowledge about Watergate).

The problem of incredulity and disbelief on the part of Americans in the word of their own Government is completely bipartisan. One may joke about "buying a used car from this man"; yet a Gallup poll taken at a comparable point in time in the Lyndon Johnson Administration found that 65 per cent of those questioned also doubted that they were getting the straight story (comparative data in *New York Times*, March 7, 1971).

Public cynicism of this kind is potentially cancerous in a free society. What brought it to pass in the United States in our day? The deepening trauma of Vietnam stimulated the worst in the governmental practice of deception, up to and including secrecy about the very act of committing the nation to war. But it cannot all be blamed on Vietnam. As I noted, there is nothing new about politicians' lying to the people or at a minimum fudging the truth. At its most cynical this tradition rests on the mystique of "reason of state," according to which anything goes so long as it is in the "interests" of the state doing it—those interests of course defined by the doer of the deed. As first articulated by King Darius of Persia, "If a lie is necessary, why not speak it? We are after all after the same thing whether we lie or speak the truth: our own advantage."

It is in this spirit that diplomats are fond of quoting the famous aphorism of Sir Henry Wooten that "a diplomat is an honest man sent abroad to lie for his country." (One noted diplomat I once worked for urged on me the motto, "When in doubt tell the truth." In the way of those given to gratuitous moralizing, he was one of the slipperiest characters I have ever known.) Even the man *Time* insisted on calling "Good, grey Cordell Hull" at least once long ago did the same, and in the process came up with a revealing explanation of the phenomenon. In 1933 the United States was cautiously edging up to the League of Nations, but still talking isolationism to appease domestic critics. The story hit the *New York Herald Tribune* and provoked an immediate denial by Secretary of State Hull.

> This Government [he said] is not contemplating any change whatever in its political relations with the League. No project of such a nature has been considered or is being considered in the Department. (Press release, Department of State, September 19, 1933)

In private, however, Hull sang a different tune. On the following day he wrote to Ambassador-at-Large Norman H. Davis:

> I was obliged categorically to deny the whole thing. Whatever we may intend, it is very handicapping to have that sort of statement *given out in advance*. It defeats our every purpose, on account of certain cross-currents of sentiment here at home. (As related by Gary B. Ostrower in "American Ambassador to the League of Nations—1933: A Proposal Postponed," *International Organization*, Winter, 1971, p. 54)

Or consider Franklin Delano Roosevelt, who ran for President in 1940 on a pledge that "your boys won't be sent into any foreign wars." Oh well, that's a campaign speech, you say, and no one believes *them*. Fair enough—but then Lyndon Johnson gets exculpated for implying during the 1964 campaign that Goldwater would escalate the war against the North, whereas L. B. J. would not.

A kind of compulsive trickiness entered U.S. foreign policy with John Foster Dulles, who was responsible for much of the official U.S. rhetoric in the Cold War. With his incessant talk of "rollback" and "liberation," Dulles must take at least part of the blame for encouraging Hungarian patriots finally to rise up in 1956 in the belief that they would be helped by the United States. Instead they were bloodily crushed by Soviet tanks in the streets of Budapest, Mr. Dulles having lost no time in assuring Moscow, in a speech at Dallas, Texas, that the United States would *not* intervene. That decision was right, but the Dulles performance downright sinful.

Or take the announcement, soon after Mr. Dulles assumed office, of the "unleashing" of Chiang Kai-shek. Yet when two years later Chiang was challenged over the off-shore islands of Quemoy and Matsu, Dulles urged restraint and privately told Chiang to knock it off. At the Geneva Conference of 1954 on Vietnam, Dulles publicly proclaimed a hard-line position while privately preparing the way for a compromise. In 1956, by publicly condemning Nasser for nationalizing the Suez Canal Company and accepting Soviet aid (after we had cut off U.S. aid, by the way), he inadvertently encouraged Britain and France to believe that they would have U.S. support in overthrowing Nasser. When they then decided on their calamitous attack, Dulles left them stunned by divorcing himself completely from their plans—which, by the way, I think was absolutely the right thing to do; but he still should have informed them clearly beforehand just where he stood. (See Louis L. Gerson and Robert J. Bresler, *John Foster Dulles* [New York: Cooper Square, 1967]; Vol. XVII of the series American Secretaries of State and Their Diplomacy.)

I cannot resist recalling another revealing episode involving Secretary Dulles that complicated my own, far more junior, official life. In 1953 Dulles addressed the American Bar Association and called on its members and all other American organizations to consider how to rewrite the U.N. Charter, revision of which was automatically to come up in the United Nations on its tenth anniversary in 1955. In his speech Dulles argued that the veto in the Security Council was strangling the organization, and implied that the door was open to drastic revision in that rule (which had been a condition for original U.S. membership in the United Nations).

My then chief, Assistant Secretary Robert Murphy, took me with him to seek clarification from the Secretary, since one of my assignments at the time was to organize U.S. preparations for the "Charter Review" item in the United Nations. Dulles, who had just unleashed thousands of earnest and well-meaning Americans on a veritable orgy of conferences, studies, and proposals on revising the U.N. Charter and getting rid of the veto, seemed surprised that we took his speech seriously. I was confused and persisted, "But Mr. Secretary, about the veto—." "Oh," he said, with his doubtless unintended sneer, "nothing can be done about the veto. As a matter of fact, we may need it some day ourselves." And, in what was to my knowledge the only critical comment he ever made about McCarthyism (which was even then shattering his own Department), he added casually, "Suppose the United Nations gets it into its head to come and investigate McCarthyism in this country?"

He dropped the subject. But the machine ground on with me at the wheel and the unwitting gullible out there in Civic Dutyland knocking themselves out. I am glad to say that at the next session of the General Assembly I managed, with the conspiratorial help of advisers from two friendly and influential delegations, to save Mr. Dulles from himself by contributing to the quiet sabotage of the agenda item he himself had already undermined while publicly touting it.

Beware a zealot in politics or diplomacy. If he is really a canny politician like Dulles, he will simply confound his friends while gratifying his enemies. If he is not a hypocrite, he will operate from Cloud Nine like our first advocate of flower power in politics, William Jennings Bryan, who preached love—hardly a bad thing—but along with it some rather inappropriate and politically unviable policies. In both cases, as Mark Twain put it, "To do good is noble. To tell others to do good is also noble and a lot less trouble."

If I seem to lean particularly hard on Mr. Dulles, it is because I think his quality of massive hypocrisy was even more damaging for the United States than his policy of massive retaliation. But if he practiced deception, so in lesser measure did the pragmatic young Galahad who soon afterward became the arbiter of U.S. foreign policy. John F. Kennedy by no means took the American public into his confidence on important foreign policy matters, but instead often treated them with the same manipulative contempt. His Administration originally claimed that it had nothing to do with the American-trained, financed, and launched invasion of Cuba at the Bay of Pigs in the spring of 1961. He even had poor Adlai Stevenson stake his considerable reputation for probity on this lie at the United Nations, making him look not only dishonest but stupid in the face of overwhelming evidence that it was a U.S. operation from start to finish.

This sort of thing is of course standard for small raids or probes that a government sensibly may want to disavow in order to avoid having either to take the blame or to follow up with its whole might if the probe fails. It was a good thing for U.S.-Latin American policy that President Kennedy stuck to this reasoning and refused to supply air cover for the invaders (which of course guaranteed their defeat). And I'm glad that in the end he had the courage to take the full blame. But the whole affair represented a scabrous episode in American history, above all as the perpetration of an international crime that irretrievably reduced the difference between America and those it criticized.

It was John F. Kennedy who firmly committed us to the Vietnam War. He did this in that same spring of 1961 (doubtless to offset the Bay of Pigs calamity and Khrushchev's chilling contempt at the Vienna Summit) by sending in four hundred Special Forces troops and a hundred other advisers and ordering a campaign of clandestine warfare against North Vietnam—*and* doing so secretly, presumably because to do it openly would constitute the first formal breach of the Geneva Agreement. (See the so-called Pentagon Papers for details.) Before his death Kennedy had authorized up to 16,000 American military personnel in Vietnam, the equivalent in numbers of a full division. But he never told the American people about the implications of this commitment, although according to some of his biographers he evidently felt it was of doubtful wisdom.

And still it continued, in season and out. Even little things got lied about. In March 1971 then Secretary of Defense Melvin Laird had to admit that a piece of pipeline exhibited at a Pentagon news conference as an example of the success of the South Vietnamese "incursion" into Laos had really been obtained during an earlier unannounced raid (*New York Times*, March 5, 1971). On December 27 and 29, 1972, Pentagon spokesman Friedheim denied that U.S. bombs had hit Hanoi's Bach Mai Hospital, despite ample visual evidence to the contrary. Such examples of official duplicity had become commonplace, despite the fact that they often turned out to have fooled not the "enemy" (who is usually very well informed) but the American people.

In 1966 the Pentagon refused for forty-four days to admit that it had lost an H-bomb over Spain, although the world was well aware of the frantic search. President Johnson first said that U.S. Marines were sent into the Dominican Republic in 1965 only to protect American lives, then caught himself up in a tangle of conflicting explanations, none of which could justify twenty thousand U.S. soldiers' occupying a neighboring state to ensure a favorable political outcome. If the Soviet's bloodless but military occupation of Czechoslovakia in 1968 for the same purpose was any different, I should like to have it explained to me.

One of the most staggering instances of deception and cover-up in the Indochina War came to light only in 1973, when it was revealed that for fourteen months prior to the U.S. invasion of ostensibly neutral Cambodia in 1970, American B-52s had been secretly bombing on a massive scale, dropping more than 100,000 tons of bombs on what were believed to be Communist supply and staging areas in Cambodia. The raids were authorized by the President but kept secret, even to the point that military reports were consistently falsified in the Pentagon's own internal reporting system, not to mention false reports to the Congress in 1971 and again in June 1973.

Perhaps there was a sound strategic reason for the bombing, given that we were in the war to defend South Vietnam. But even that judgment was obscured by the deliberate lie told to the American people by their President in announcing the April 30, 1970, invasion. With the unerring compulsion to exaggeration and untruth that tainted so many of this President's deeds, he told his people that "American policy since then [1954] has been to respect scrupulously the neutrality of the Cambodian people." He solemnly added, "For the past five years, we have provided no military assistance whatever . . . to Cambodia." Everyone concerned, save the sovereign American people and their Congress, knew the falsity of Mr. Nixon's words.

American planes flew combat support missions over Cambodia from 1970 on, despite President Nixon's assurance that they would not do so. And a heavy-footed succession of Pentagon statements, denials, and admissions attended the massive bombing of North Vietnamese targets at the time of the futile Sontay prison camp raid in November 1970 (and most bombings of North Vietnam that followed), all in possible violation of the "Understanding" of October 31, 1968. (Numerous such episodes are chronicled by Anthony Lake in "Lying Around Washington" in *Foreign Policy*, Spring 1971, pp. 91–113.)

It seems possible that serious negotiations in 1971-72 on Vietnam were adversely affected by what was later revealed as systematic duplicity on the part of U.S. theater commanders in deliberately planning North Vietnam bombing raids and publicly reporting them as "protective reaction," which was always understood to mean defensive firing after being targeted by enemy aircraft or radar, but which in this case was deliberately misused. Air Force General John D. Lavelle was demoted for that violation of Presidential policy. It was President Nixon, however, who bombed Hanoi and mined Haiphong in the spring of 1972 in response to Hanoi's massive new invasion of South Vietnam, and presented it to the American people as an act in defense of the departing American ground troops. Yet it was clearly designed, as Johnson's bombing had been, to terrorize North Vietnam into modifying its aims in the South.

I myself believe that Hanoi committed both a crime and a blunder in mounting a new invasion in early 1972 while U.S. ground forces were departing, and thus justifying at least some U.S. retaliation. No justification could be found for the punitive bombing campaign of Hanoi over Christmas 1972 following U.S. attempts to change the peace terms agreed to in October, and this time no effort at all was made to explain to the American people. Both instances furnished new reasons why (as Mr. Nixon had said three months earlier) "Some of our citizens have become accustomed to thinking that whatever our government says must be false, and whatever our enemies say must be true" (*New York Times*, January 26, 1972).

An accompanying evil, lesser but nonetheless deplorable, is the corruption of language that accompanies such corruption of thought. For language, if we are to believe the semanticists, expresses both outer and inner thoughts. To avoid the truth you may twist the meaning of words, but in the process you twist yourself a bit. All wars produce new jargon, but the Vietnam War produced an anti-jargon. "Protective reaction" became a game played at Pentagon briefings, with no one present laboring under the illusion that it stood for anything but an aerial rocket or bombing attack on North Vietnam. In Laos we didn't invade, we "incurred." When that didn't work out as announced, we executed a "mobile maneuver" (which Senator Fulbright with some but not total exaggeration described as Pentagonese for "headlong retreat"). The ill-fated Sontay raid to rescue U.S. prisoners, in addition to a flat lie (later confessed) denying any related air raids, produced "appropriate ordnance" and "diversionary activity" to describe the bombing, when admitted (*New York Times*, November 27, 1970). The euphemism perhaps most widely derided was Presidential News Secretary Ronald Ziegler's dematerialization of previous Presidential denials about White House Watergate involvement as "inoperative."

The habit will never be faced and dealt with, however, if lying to escape public criticism is not distinguished from the necessity of a reasonable privacy in the normal conduct of foreign affairs and national security. It was an absurd exaggeration to urge, as did Daniel Ellsberg and some others involved with the Pentagon Papers, that *all* government secrets be henceforth shared with the reading public. Any chance of peace settlements in the Middle East, or détente with China or Russia, would go up in smoke if that advice were followed. I can think of a whole agenda of peacemaking efforts that, as with information about troopships full of men, fully justify privacy and evasion.

I shall go farther and argue that no national or international interest is served by admitting that one is engaged in spying, particularly when the spying is to reassure oneself that no military surprises are being secretly prepared. The chances of avoiding nuclear war will be greatly reinforced to the extent that the United States, Russia, China, and any other nuclear power obtain such continual reassurance, by whatever means, a point clearly recognized in the 1972 SALT Agreement and in other arms control agreements calling for verification by "national means." In 1960, when Francis Gary Powers was shot down in his U-2 high-altitude flight over the Soviet Union, Washington claimed that he was only collecting weather data. It may be necessary to disavow your intelligence agents—except that in this case Moscow had carefully collected both the crashed plane and Mr. Powers. The outcome was that President Eisenhower blurted out the whole truth, and in the process scuttled the 1960 Paris summit conference.

It is generally accepted that wartime military operations may legitimately be kept secret, on the ground that lives are needlessly jeopardized by blabbing (although I never heard of a single major allied military operation in Vietnam, year after year, which was not obviously "blown" in advance). The traditional spirit here is expressed in Stonewall Jackson's famous formula, "Mystify, mislead, and surprise." The best examples of its application in recent U.S. history are D-Day in 1945 and MacArthur's Inchon landing in Korea in 1950.

I am even willing to accept a state of permanent tension between the ravenous—and gloriously free—American press, and those charged with keeping proper secrets secret. President Kennedy's Special Assistant McGeorge Bundy thus congratulated Presidential Press Secretary Pierre Salinger in 1963 on a memo Salinger had written:

> Pierre: Champion! Excellent Prose. No Surprise. A communiqué should say nothing in such a way as to fool the press without deceiving them. (Revealed in the opening of the Kennedy Files by the J. F. Kennedy Presidential Library. See *New York Times*, August 1, 1971)

The only trouble was that the subject was a deliberately vague press communiqué written by Salinger after a Cabinet-level review of the Vietnam situation held in Honolulu in November 1963; and its deliberate vagueness was part of the pervasive effort by that and the following Administration to play down the growing American involvement in Vietnam. In context Bundy's aphorism strikes me as too clever by half.

Why make a Federal case out of all this? Why not just accept it as the normal "protective reaction" of bureaucrats and politicians, a well-understood expression of their age-old fear of being criticized and their incapacity to admit error? The reasons for not doing so are twofold. The first is pragmatic. Lying rarely works, as Abraham Lincoln pointed out when he said that "No man has a good enough memory to be a successful liar." The greatest mystery of all is why any reasonably intelligent public figure bothers to twist and writhe to avoid telling something that practically everyone is aware of. As James Reston wrote, it was not that any recent administration was successful in concealing its tricks:

> On the contrary, they have been deceitful, clumsy, and unsuccessful, and even after the Pentagon papers, and the Anderson papers, the reaction seems to be not that they were wrong and deceptive, but that they were caught. (*New York Times*, January 8, 1972)

Because for all that diplomacy specializes in indirection, deliberate ambiguity and white lies—often for good and sufficient reason—a powerful truth resides in the conclusion of the great French diplomat, Jules Cambon, that "the most persuasive method at the disposal of a government is the word of an honest man" (quoted by Harold Nicolson in *Diplomacy* [London: Oxford University Press, 1963], p. 57).

The other negative consequence of habitual evasion is not pragmatic but moral (and in the end, as with political morality in general, intensely practical). The covenant between the people and their democratically-elected government is a fragile one. It can be gravely bruised by giving power to demagogues like Huey Long or Joe McCarthy or George Wallace, because such men do not play by the rules but work on the nation's jugular, which is a very vulnerable piece of political anatomy. For some strange reason people will actively co-operate for a time in appeals to their basest instincts. But demagogues don't last long in a free country, thank God.

The delicate mechanism of trust may also be eroded by well-meaning, highly educated, and selfless men who confuse their temporary power with a monopoly of superior wisdom. To my mind this, rather than any conspiratorial plot, economic drive, or class interest accounted for the evils of arrogance, closed-mindedness, and concealment from public scrutiny that came to infect the basically decent people who have operated the machinery of American foreign policy in recent years.

I often wonder why a President cannot decide that it might just turn out to be more profitable to him politically, and far more beneficial to the country he serves, to abandon the endless game of fudging the truth, along with the bruising warfare with the Congress over secret Executive agreements instead of open treaties and the scramble to put the best face on everything including error and failure. What would happen if at its topmost levels the U.S. Government, just as an experiment, decided to tell the truth (and if not, then simply to say "No comment")?

Of all the experiments tried in American politics in recent years—"packaging candidates," "merchandising policies," "selling America abroad," and all the rest—the only one never tried was simply leveling with the people. Some illustrative examples I would have appreciated: "It turned out that Bosch's election would *not* have meant a Communist takeover in Santo Domingo"; or "Aerial bombing doesn't really compel surrender when the people are united"; or, "We didn't know how to fight against guerrillas—and we still don't"; or, "We've hurt a lot of innocent people in Indochina"; or, "If it were my territory the Israelis occupied I'd do everything I could to get it back"; or, "I guess I never noticed until very late that China and Russia had split up"; or, "It was stupid to use up all that American prestige fighting to keep Peking out of the UN"; or, "We blamed Taiwan's ouster on the United Nations but it was really our doing in bringing Peking in"; or, "I bombed Hanoi and Haiphong in 1972–73 not because it had anything to do with U.S. troop withdrawals but because I wanted to show Moscow (Peking, Hanoi, etc.) I could be tough and unpredictable"; or, "Let's stop expecting poor and hungry people to be grateful for foreign aid"; or . . . or . . . or. . . .

It is hard to disagree with Mr. Lake's conclusion: "Not to be believed—the present condition—threatens the character of representative democracy. Even the strongest democratic government on earth must be gravely damaged if its own citizens do not believe it." It has to be said, by one who did not necessarily oppose all the things we did, that this is a form of corruption capable of dissolving the cement that binds the American people and those in whom they place some of their precious trust. It is a vicious habit, and the politicians and the bureaucrats had better try very hard to kick it before all confidence in government is lost.

The model is General J. W. ("Vinegar Joe") Stilwell, whose classic statement after being driven out of Burma by the Japanese, "I claim we got a hell of a beating," will be remembered and honored long after all the dodges and protective reactions and cover-ups have found the permanent obscurity they so richly deserve.

Perils of Power

The U.S. Department of State contains some of the brightest people I have ever worked with—and that includes the Charles River Gang, of which I am now a member. But it is nothing short of notorious how deadening to the spirit of needful change *any* bureaucratic apparatus can be. Mao Tse-tung could well have had this in mind when he launched his Cultural Revolution from above. The revolution was full of excesses, including some vile behavior toward their elders and betters by millions of hopped-up youths. But Chairman Mao probably felt the way outgoing President Truman said incoming President Eisenhower would feel. Truman wrote, "He'll sit here and he'll say, 'Do this!' 'Do that!'

And nothing will happen " (Richard Neustadt in *Presidential Power* [New York: New American Library, 1964], p. 22).

Inside government there is not much *open* dissent from the premises that have driven U.S. foreign policy; and that is as it should be. Intellectuals lionized Daniel Ellsberg when he admitted to having purloined and turned over to several newspapers classified government documents bearing on the Vietnam War. At first I was shocked. After signing quite a few solemn oaths over the years acknowledging the Draconian penalties for betraying secrets given to me in confidence, I was not prepared to accept Ellsberg as the final arbiter of this particular morality. I later came to acknowledge the usefulness—as a single, one-time, convulsive act—of that massive uncovering of the inner government mind as it made judgments affecting the fate of us all without seeming to consult either human values or the spirit of the United States Constitution. But if this becomes a frequent practice there can be no government and no foreign policy.

It is curious and disappointing that more high officials who privately complained of their deep alienation from Presidential policy did not resign and speak their convictions publicly. The reasons given are many, most of them sounding like cop-outs. Professor Patricia Harris told friends, after she had resigned as Dean of Howard University Law School over a disagreement on principle, that one reason she did so was that when she had previously been in government (as a U.S. delegate to the United Nations) she had become fed up with whose who said in whispers, "I'd resign in a minute but of course I can do more if I stay in." More recently Elliot Richardson won enormous public respect for resigning on principle from the Attorney Generalship.

On a more superficial level, occasionally a government official *does* bespeak the need to break out of old fetters. Admiral Elmo Zumwalt made himself the Charles Reich of the U.S. Defense Establishment when, on taking over as Chief of Naval Operations at the unprecedented youthful age of 47, he told critics of his personnel reforms:

> It is time for us to withdraw our heads from the sands. . . . The time is long since past when we can wrap ourselves in the comfortable memories of life in a simpler age, hoping that traditional solutions alone will work against modern problems. . . . The Navy has reached a point where we can no longer drift with the tides and winds of change totally oblivious to the demands of our youth, the needs of our civilian society. . . . What is needed are men with vision, imagination, and above all, understanding of what is going on in the world around them. (New York Times, June 10, 1971)

In the Navy this meant primarily scrapping the sailor suits with their infantile trouser flaps, as well as serving beer and letting the hair grow longer, but entailed also crackdowns on racist ship commanders. Secretary of State Kissinger made a comparable plea on taking office in 1973. He too faced a bureaucracy laden with not only tradition, but also with a decade of failure caused at least in part by the pre-emption of foreign policy activity by Dr. Kissinger's own White House staff.

During the late 1960s there was an interesting reform movement within the State Department system—more precisely the Foreign Service—led by a group known as the "Young Turks," a covey of bright and discontented junior Foreign Service Officers who decided to do the unthinkable and seize power within the system in order to shake it up. By working within the system they of course accepted many of its preconditions, including several of the key premises under which U.S. foreign policy operates. Their rebellious mood was thus ridiculed by some outsiders to whom their very willingness to serve meant that they were fatally "co-opted." Actually, some did share significantly in the wave of reform-mindedness that swept over much of the non-governmental "foreign policy community." But it was also true that their approach was that of technicians, focusing on archaic practices in running the foreign policy machine. Here their chief enemy was the resistance of many of their seniors to using methods of analysis and planning that had revolutionized much of American business, not to mention State's great five-sided policy rival across the Potomac.

The Young Turks were motivated also by awareness of how low the State Department had slipped in the policy ladder. They were thus anxious to reverse the humiliating trend toward denigrating as unimaginative, excessively cautious, or late, so many of the State Department's views and policy proposals, a trend that had started with President Franklin D. Roosevelt. In more recent times, beginning with President Kennedy, the trend steadily grew despite occasional attempts by State to reassert its prerogatives. From that time to the naming of Henry Kissinger as Secretary of State the White House staff insisted that it *wanted* State to pick up its responsibilities, but "it just doesn't seem able to." Walt Rostow said this three months after he and McGeorge Bundy took over as Mr. Kennedy's chief assistants. A decade later, Presidential assistants didn't bother even to explain that they were trying to get State to do its job. They simply acted as though responsibility for the more crucial foreign policy operations had been transferred to the National Security Council staff.

After their unprecedented election as a slate to the Board of the American Foreign Service Association, leaders of the Young Turks sought outside support in their efforts to bring the State Department into the second half of the twentieth century. Lannon Walker, the newly elected Board Chairman, and Charles Bray, later to become the Department's press spokesman, met with a small group of us in Boston to outline their strategy. I was particularly excited by their efforts, since this could mean a revival of the Department's moribund policy-planning apparatus, as well as the introduction of valuable (but scorned) aids to policy such as computers to assist the fallible human memory, and mind-stretching simulation exercises—to name only two. While some in the administrative and research branches of the State Department did manage to insinuate a few of the more modern methods into the building, these appeared to me to have had little or no real support from senior officers on the policy side, particularly after Elliot Richardson left the post of Under Secretary.

What seemed to block this modest effort was an attitude of unshakeable assurance that old-fashioned intuition and sound judgment were all that was needed—an attitude combined with skittishness about being caught in bed, as it were, with the exotic and unfamiliar gimmickry of modern social science. In 1958, on my first return visit to Washington in company with my new M.I.T. colleagues Max Millikan and Walt Rostow, the then Acting Secretary of State Christian Herter said that he was interested in having State Department planning officers participate in my new "political games" based on Rand Corporation experiments in the mid-1950s. This "games" device, which at Millikan's urging I had just begun to develop, seemed a promising way to anticipate better some of the crises that surprised us earlier in the Government. But at the time, Congressman John Rooney of Brooklyn dominated the life of the State Department—and, as Secretary Herter explained, Mr. Rooney would never understand the Department's "playing games"; Mr. Herter ruled that while the Department must never so expose itself, some of its officers should come to M.I.T. instead.

In 1961 the Pentagon set up the Joint War Games Agency, and thenceforth Department officers *did* take part in their games as well as in ours at M.I.T. In 1963, under the goad of those two unorthodox Assistant Secretaries of State, G. Mennen ("Soapy") Williams and Walt Rostow, the Department organized a full-dress, senior-level political planning game in-house (which I directed). But apart from some rather marginal efforts since—all remote from the policy core—I am not aware of any other such exercises on the premises. Thanks to the initiative of the Young Turks, however, a series of internal studies was undertaken, with result in a massive set of State Department Task Force Reports containing recommendations which, if fully implemented, would convert the Department into a very modern structure indeed. The record of implementation so far is spotty.

One thing that continues to worry me, moreover, is the unlikelihood that government can provide internally the kind of challenges that will really probe underlying policy, *unless such a process is built into the machinery itself.* In perhaps the most felicitously written memoir to come from the pen of a former Assistant Secretary of State, Columbia Professor Charles Frankel described the frame of mind that excludes for all practical purposes the very challenging of assumptions and of familiar patterns of policy that is most needed.

> The life of an official does not merely turn him aside from more spacious reflections; it creates in him professional habits and a kind of professional pride which lead him to believe that reality is where the nitty-gritty is, that policy isn't made by the great thinkers but by tough men who take each problem as it comes and do the best they can with it. (*High on Foggy Bottom* [New York: Harper & Row, 1968–69], p. 85–86)

One consequence of this demanding (and heady) sense of day-to-day responsibility is demonstrably to stifle the impulse for reform, or at least to ensure that changes are purely marginal. Many within government have become aware of this institutional shortcoming, though baffled as to how it ought to be treated. A 1970 Airlie House conference organized by the State Department, the International Studies Association, and the American Foreign Service Association provided a rare occasion for diplomats, bureaucrats, politicians, and intellectuals to confront this range of problems. It became painfully clear that each plays such a different role as to preclude agreement on what is real, let alone what is "do-able."

The intellectuals seemed to be looking for new ideas, placed positive value on change for the sake of renewal of the national spirit, and positively enjoyed their feeling of boldness. Their favorite phrase was, "*Why can't* we urge the following. . . ?"—after which they would sketch out a change of U.S. direction at least 45 degrees off the present course (if not 90 or even 180).

The government officials present, particularly those with current operational or diplomatic responsibilities, automatically came up with objections to any proposal of change. Their style was that of the lawyer rehearsing all the conceivable questions his client was likely to be asked in court. It was part game, part ingrained ability to see every argument and so find the only true safety in immobility. Their conclusion, to no one's surprise, was a chronic preference for the known status quo—unsatisfactory as that may be—to the uncertainties of some undiscovered country from whose bourn no bureaucrat gets promoted. The syndrome is painfully familiar, and one could even see the validity of the arguments. But making an ironclad principle out of a useful caution is wrong and even dangerous.

Another familiar quality of my old State Department friends that bedevils U.S. policy emerged at that meeting just as it does in real-life diplomatic conferences. It is to find "solutions"—if substantive consensus proves difficult—through *drafting*. This process is a chief reason for such diplomatic time bombs as the Yalta Agreement, in which clever drafting of agreed words was used to paper over grave substantive disagreements. The give-away phrase is "Wouldn't the following language take care of it?" Sometimes it does; but the verbal gimmick all too easily becomes the reality and, like a Chinese meal, leaves one feeling deceptively satisfied.

In decrying the militaristic bent that seemed to infect civilian policy thinking, I suggested above that the price for desirable diplomatic caution might be the inertia for which the State Department has been attacked. Perhaps we should accept that price. Moreover, as Lawrence Durrell wrote, by way of explaining the pigheadedness of his British colleagues in the colonial Cyprus he described so hauntingly, "It is absurd to expect the qualities of ballet dancers in public servants or to despair when one doesn't find them" (*Bitter Lemons* [London: Faber and Faber, 1957], p. 153).

What is needed is not dancers but choreographers. If every

State Department policy official is, by definition, an *ex officio* policy-planner, then ingrained caution is not enough. For nothing is more certain than that this particular cast of mind is not going to be very hospitable to my own definition of the "planning approach," which involves putting responsible challenges to underlying assumptions that have tended to govern our international behavior for three decades. The aim is to develop better policies. But at the moment it would be adequate just to be sure that we understand what we really believe we are doing. And it is still an unsettled issue whether there is a realistic way to loosen up fixed premises and beliefs sufficiently to put the nation on a significantly improved course as we careen through this revolutionary century.

Consider the reports of conversations during early 1972 within the Washington Special Action Group (WSAG) that were spread before the public by columnist Jack Anderson concerning the U.S. role in the 1971 India-Pakistan war over East Pakistan. It certainly sounded as though any time the officials appointed to advise on such matters even began to question the premises of U.S. policy, instant censure ensued from Dr. Kissinger, to the point of threats that, if the State Department did not conform, its functions would be taken over by the White House. I myself took no pleasure in seeing one of the most intelligent men I know apparently suspend *his* judgment because his boss had cracked the whip. And yet no one with even moderate delusions of being Otto von Bismarck could willingly have chosen Pakistan's side in that conflict.

Another example concerns U.S. policy toward a European Security Conference and a conference on mutual reduction of military forces in Europe. Isn't it just a little arrogant to assume, as U.S. policy seems to, that any substantial withdrawal of U.S. ground forces from Europe would see the Western Europeans simply crumble and become "Finlandized"? Why do we assume that the Europeans don't understand their own vital interests?

How sound is our governing premise that Western Europeans would do nothing to correct for any U.S. withdrawal because they "really don't understand the Soviet threat"? Do we really believe that they are that stupid and uninformed? In any case, how do we know that our estimate of that threat is necessarily correct?

A partial answer came on a visit to NATO headquarters outside Brussels in the course of research on European Security questions. Among the old acquaintances I visited was one with important policy responsibilities. At one point I asked how he had used the outcome of that extraordinary political-military exercise at Garmisch mentioned in the first part of this essay. He told me that he "paid absolutely no attention to such things," considering them "not important." So much for the planning efforts that *do* take place. How are we *ever* to get the challenging questions asked? And—more to the point—how do we get them asked by those with serious professional concerns and responsibilities, rather than just by the hostile, the alienated, or the enemies of the system?

There is no dearth of organizations claiming to operate efficiently and evaluate options systematically. But at a more primary level, where one rethinks underlying assumptions, makes detached appraisals of the situation, and re-examines long-held approaches—in short, does basic policy planning—the State Department planning function has been drastically curtailed, and there is no evidence that this essential task is being performed elsewhere.

In the final chapter of this book I have laid out some lines of thought that I hope can help restore to foreign policy both internal coherence and external creativity. Without changes in attitudes toward the premises and purposes of foreign policy, however, there seems to me little hope of improvement in either our morale or our historic reputation. In such case, tinkering with policy machinery would be an evasion. But with such changes—and perhaps as a way to help keep official perspectives imaginative and unstereotyped—one structural reform commends itself: the creation of a quasi-independent and influential long- and middle-range policy planning staff whose aim would be to help restore the balance by supplying the continuous built-in challenges and organized mind-stretching that are needed to get us on to new, higher ground. That is what the busy, operational, and parochial bureaucracies of government need most and enjoy least. Such a staff must be set up within government, and set up in ways the operators will respect for the reason that it is well-informed and backed up by the enthusiastic support of the President and Secretary of State.

Above all, this staff would supply to goverment what is missing in the system, as former White House Secretary George Reedy has pointed out—a "procedure for adversary political debate in determining policy" ("The Personal Touch," *New York Times*, July 1, 1971, Op-Ed page).

It is no longer a secret that most major U.S. policy decisions regarding the Vietnam War from *circa* 1960 ran contrary to the advice of the intelligence community. The ability of leaders to ignore the findings of impartial, loyal observers, or to dismiss their implications as "speculative," suggests the need for a quasi-independent appraisal of intelligence information against the kinds of options policy-makers think they face. This is simply not done by a committee of venerable high-level government advisers such as we now have reviewing the quality of intelligence operations. As with the policy-planning function, the value of an independent intelligence appraisal would be to insert into the rolling policy consensus the views and analyses that are today missing. The English worked out something like this, although different in detail, in setting up an "Assessments Office" attached to the Prime Minister, headed up by an extremely able former head of policy planning in the Foreign Office. Subsequently Prime Minister Heath set up a "think tank" known as the General Policy Review Staff to make semi-independent periodic reviews, using analytical tools, of governmental strategy.

All in all, a clear need can be demonstrated for a new structure that enables policy planning to function in ways impossible to squash or suppress, including inputs from vital sectors of American society still basically excluded from foreign policy decision-making. This structure should not be placed in the State Department, since strong secretaries cannot be always assumed. It should not be exclusively in the White House, where it would have to conform to a President's preferences. It cannot be totally outside government, for then it would have no clout. It cannot be located in the Congress, for there it would be presumed to have a permanently antagonistic role.

My concept is that of a quasi-independent agency reporting to the President but responsible to the Congress, like the General Accounting Office. If this is too grandiose for the modest task of thinking, perhaps a quasi-independent agency of the Executive Branch—like the Arms Control and Disarmament Agency (but stronger)—nominally under the Secretary of State but with statutory access to the President. Or perhaps a body headed by an Under Secretary of State with a concurrent appointment as Special Assistant to the President, along the lines of the 1973 designation of Henry Kissinger to be Secretary of State while continuing to be the Number One White House adviser.

That staff would do many of the things good policy planners were to do in the State Department: talk, think, initiate studies on long-term implications that busy operators worry about but don't have time for, and on topics operators rarely focus upon. (The motto for that last might well be Harvard Professor Thomas Schelling's mind-blowing question, "How do you make a list of things you would never have thought of?") In addition, they would take the best of techniques already available (e.g., gaming, simulation, forecasting exercises, computer modeling) but often feared, scorned, or misunderstood as substitutes for thinking—which of course they are not. Finally, by flexible use of outsiders they would artificially inseminate the policy machinery with "extra-Establishment" views notoriously lacking in the consensus-ridden bureaucracies (but invaluable to the President if only he realized it).

★ ★ ★ ★

When all is said and done, it is the President who is charged by the Constitution with the conduct of U.S. foreign policy, limited only by those few powers specifically granted to the Senate and the House. And while he certainly is not going to dissent from his own policies, at best it is the President who *does* sometimes challenge antiquated assumptions and who *does* try to turn the nation in new directions. President Kennedy, for all that he was a thoroughly committed Cold Warrior, undermined some of his own policy premises with his extraordinary American University speech calling for revising many ingrown attitudes toward the Cold War.

President Nixon in his dazzling turnaround of U.S. China policy showed how a thoroughly pragmatic political tactician can, at *his* best, get at the heart of a policy that needs uprooting. Curiously enough, it was that other master tactician, President Lyndon B. Johnson, who committed himself to a set of Vietnam propositions from which he could not disengage himself, and as to which he would brook no challenge from others.*

Much of the domestic debate about both Vietnam and Watergate had to do with the vastly increased power of the U.S. Presidency. Other nations may not like us or want to do our bidding. Still, the President *is*, in material terms, the "most powerful man

---

* I recall with acute discomfort the argument I made in favor of Mr. Johnson's election in 1964. Some Cambridge colleagues used the threat of a Goldwater escalation in the Vietnam War to take me out of my determined non-partisanship, and I wound up moderating a large public meeting in which the panel of speakers consisted of several of the top scientific advisers to a whole series of American Presidents. Apart from cracking my whip and telling jokes, my own substantive contribution was, as befits a political scientist, to explain that it was Senator Johnson's very qualities as a practical, hard-bitten politician that the nation needed to keep our world role flexible and pragmatic. I haven't been lured out of my Independent shell since.

in the world." He disposes of the military capacity to blow them (and us) up, and he has substantial control over the role played in the world by America's phenomenal material wealth. Alongside this increase in power (and, by definition, responsibility) has been the growth in what can only be called the monarchical aspects of the Presidency, in the form of accoutrements and facilities no President had before, say, 1950. The personal jets and helicopters, the resplendent White House ceremonial guard, the vast proliferation of direct White House control over diplomatic and economic policy, the instant access to two hundred million souls simply by bringing the TV cameras into the Oval Room. All this, as George Reedy pointed out in his sobering recollections, has the effect of making the job essentially unmanageable, in an atmosphere increasingly resembling that of a fantastically powerful monarchy. (Watergate showed how that power can corrupt.)

Under the circumstances, how can a President possibly react the way other Americans do? How can he get the feel of criticism? How can he sense that some of his own basic convictions need overhauling? Mr. Nixon got up at 5 A.M. on May 9, 1970, the day of a march on Washington of young war protesters, and drove to the Lincoln Memorial where, according to the newspapers, he talked for an hour with five dissident students. It seemed an extraordinary effort on the President's part to communicate. But the five, according to subsequent accounts, were stunned for a different reason. "He talked to us about *football*," one exclaimed in astonishment. The rest of the time he "explained his policies" to them.

Mr. Nixon's later-disclosed confusion of domestic policy dissent with street violence and foreign espionage could be explained at least in part by this failure to listen, if only out of curiosity, to what was being said, in order to understand what was obsessing huge numbers in the next generation. For any public official it is considered normal to try to "sell" official policy. But one of our deepest national wounds inevitably went unhealed so long as those at the top did not just for once shut up, open their minds and hearts, and try very hard to get the feel of that alien, alienated, incomprehensible agony of the disaffected.

This phenomenon of President-as-monarch came home to me vividly as a guest at a White House State dinner a couple of years ago. Of course, it is common politeness to defer or to mute one's critical impulses. It is natural to be awed. It is simply a routine to impress the guests for the President and the First Lady to sweep down the stairs preceeded by a four-man color guard to the strains of "Hail to the Chief." And they don't eat off gold service every day (or do they?). Agreed, he could not do his job so well if he had to do more than press a button when he decides to helicopter to another place, where he will be received equally regally. As a simple, awestruck taxpayer, however, I was impressed anew, as others must be, to *see* the President in his ceremonial and professional setting, in the solemnity and majesty of that position regardless of who occupies it—a setting in which dignity, formality, and the accommodation of his slightest personal whim go along with the agenda of massive national and international problems upon which he must make decisions for this country.

It was driven home powerfully that even if a President really *wants* to know how minorities feel, or how poor urban slum-dwellers live, or how dissident students react, all he can do, apart from an occasional quick inspection trip with all of *its* paraphernalia, is to hear about it in that same setting of grandeur, awesome responsibility, and institutional deference. As Russell Baker once put it, "If Nixon had to ride the railroad to San Clemente, California, like people do, instead of flying in his own private superjetliner, railroad service would soon be fit for human consumption again" (*New York Times*, January 28, 1971). The very description of the Presidency as "lonely" is a dead give-away.

In our system the President is both Chief of State and head of government. Many of the ceremonial trappings belong to the first role. But as head of government he is, unlike presidents in many other systems, answerable only to the electorate, and that only every four years. Unlike prime ministers he is never answerable to the Legislative Branch; and with his operations still protected by "executive privilege," there remains no one to whom he can be held accountable at the time of fateful Presidential decisions. Even press conferences are a poor substitute, both because they are held only when a President wants, and also because the press has its own newsmaking fish to fry.

The night in question we dined under a portrait of President Lincoln I had never seen before—smiling wryly, informally posed, human in every detail. But even Abraham Lincoln, with his deep sense of common humanity, would have trouble today acquiring the *feel* of these outside tides and currents and passions, encapsulated and isolated as he too would be in the elaborate and shielded apparatus of the twentieth-century presidency.

PRESCRIPTION

★ 5 ★

THE LIGHT AT THE END OF THE TUNNEL

The Boundaries of Change

In redefining the United States' world role the most essential ingredient is a set of altered attitudes on the part of policy officials and those to whom they should be able to look for support and understanding. Important changes in policy will flow logically from changed perspectives. But in some other areas the United States will legitimately find itself doing much the same as before.

In distinguishing between the two, what has to be confronted is to be found neither in cost-benefit calculations nor at the level of diplomatic style and maneuver where a Bismarck competes with Wilsonians. Beneath all that, the deepest tensions in our body politic concern conflicting beliefs about the nature of man and the meaning of morality in public policy. The contradictions in American foreign policy reflect this underlying tragedy of the human condition. At the root of both is an unresolved clash between values and power, between the divine spark of humanity and the tyranny of autonomous systems. In our age the result is tension and collision at every level between the spiritual, compassionate side of man and the complex, non-human systems he has created for his social, economic, and political life. This is no philosophical abstraction. The choices to be made between policies arise from the proportions one assigns to the two sides of the equation.

More than seventy years ago Henry Adams wrote of the same dilemma in the chapter of his "Education" captioned "The Virgin and the Dynamo." Today the same value clash finds the humane "reverence for life" (Albert Schweitzer's distillation of his abiding love for man) in desperate tension with organization, management, and system. In our epoch the battles so far are invariably won not by man but by systems. Modernization is making materialists of the "spiritual" cultures, and post-industrialization is filling the advanced societies with walking wounded. The visible modern dropouts are only the tip of an iceberg of souls who feel themselves shriveled and humiliated by unfulfilling work, unreachable corporate bodies of business, labor, education, government, and computerized warfare. In world politics the result can approach the genocidal. "Scientific" socialists wind up incarcerating whole populations in the name of equality, while liberal democracies find themselves in bloody crusades in the name of diversity and freedom of choice. With the failure of so many gods, the urge is strong to put a plague on all houses.

But I cling to the belief that dropping out is not just another way of bettering man's condition, and that is what still interests me as a goal. Edmund Burke was historically accurate when he said that "the only thing necessary for the triumph of evil is for good men to do nothing." A reformed foreign policy for the United States, far from escaping the tension between humanity and system, needs to become more explicit about it.

Liberal American foreign policy implied gradualism, belief in human progress, defense against imperialistic power drives, and a quest for co-operative international structures. It was even historically logical for the United States, as a super-rich and super-strong continental power, to favor stability and equilibrium in the world beyond its borders. But in our times this preference went out of bounds to support for the status quo in detail, a feeling of omniscience, undifferentiated counterrevolution, economic greed, and fascination with operating the system itself. The words of liberalism remained, but the spirit was betrayed by both men and events.

In seeking remedies it became customary recently to ask what our options are. The difficulty with this is that what seems available may be inconsistent with what is desirable. This defect in the options game flows in turn from the time lag that seems to condemn our larger national responses to perpetual obsolescence. In fact, analysis of the last few decades, and of the American attitude toward the great tidal forces of world history, leads this author to suggest something that might be called the "decade lag." Perhaps it even has the stature of a "law." It holds that in modern times the United States in each new decade seems finally to face up to the problems that built up in the previous period, while at the same time still newer problems go unrecognized, or unsolved even if acknowledged.

Thus, the 1930s dealt with the economic lunacies and inequalities of the 1920s—*after* the great Crash. Thus, the 1940s confronted the aggression and dangerous overturn of the balance of power of the 1930s—*after* Pearl Harbor awoke this nation from its drugged trip into isolationism. Thus, the 1950s produced the anti-Communism and national security doctrines of the Cold War aimed at staving off the threatening Communist monolith led by Moscow—as it was beginning to fracture.

And thus the 1960s devised programs such as Flexible Response, the Alliance for Progress, and Counter-Insurgency Doctrine—all after the reality of revolutionary change and unrest began to show how complex and blurred was the mix of economic inequality and social and political injustice with the conspiracies of "indirect aggression" and subversion that still operated. If we are lucky the 1970s will see the United States finally focus on the enormous array of unresolved domestic problems—while still newer weaknesses develop in an international order that remains fatally inadequate even for the modest jobs the nations have assigned to it.

What this lesson teaches is that to get on top of our dilemmas we cannot always accept that which the tactical situation seems to dictate, but must impose on it our best strategic vision and purposes. All the trends may point toward a new American neo-isolationism, with this country dropping out from a broad range of activities, from economic assistance to leadership in the building of new institutions. And yet both the facts of U.S. power and the norms of America's broad interests call for more rather than less involvement in those respects.

America may be currently demoralized in the face of failures, and disillusioned about the validity of its self-image. But ironically we have reason soon to move decisively to fresh "commitments," not to this or that tin-horn dictator who claims anti-Communism, but to redefined purpose, such as greater economic equality and prevention of conflict, along with such valid older stands as opposing naked military aggression. This is why isolationism is a non-policy for the United States in the 1970s, the 1980s, and until the end of the century, despite the mood of many Americans who want to put domestic problem-solving first and believe that the way to do this is to downgrade foreign affairs. Their urge to decouple America from the globalism that has turned sour is understandable. They can legitimately argue different norms than I do. But their error is in misconstruing the linkage between troubles abroad and troubles at home, which turns out to be a tricky one.

As the Bolsheviks discovered in the early 1920s (and Peking's [rul]ers after their "Cultural Revolution" of the mid-1960s), even [ra]dical change of policy at home can be accompanied by only [m]odest turn in external relations—if, that is, there are to be [any] external relations at all. Leon Trotsky is reported to have said, [when] asked to become Commissar of Soviet Foreign Affairs in [1917,] "What, are *we* to have foreign relations?" He went on to [say, "I] will publish a few revolutionary proclamations and then [sh]op." The rest, as they say, is history.

THE LIGHT AT THE END OF THE TUNNEL

The "inside" world at home may be profoundly altered, but the outside world is a dynamic system with its own constants and variables, mostly unsusceptible to manipulation by any single state, even a super-powerful one. U.S. domestic life is long overdue for some basic reforms, and U.S. foreign policies need to change to conform to altered realities and perceptions. But if the national perspective gets too much out of register with external reality, it will become as irrational and unsuitable as previous policies that led us astray.

The task is to decide afresh what is vitally important to the nation, while not abandoning our hold on external reality. We need to learn our lessons from the years of scourge, but also to bear in mind Mark Twain's injunction not to get out of an experience more than there is in it. ("A cat that sits on a hot stove won't sit on a hot stove again. But she won't sit on a cold one either.") But I would also echo former Urban Affairs Secretary George Romney, perhaps the only man in the United States or any other government honest enough to admit it, when he said "The truth is, none of us are sure what are the right things to do" (quoted in *International Herald Tribune*, March 8, 1972).

★ ★ ★ ★

A key boundary is established by the way we define our national interests. It was not very long ago that one could infer the external objectives of America by simply looking around the world and seeing what we were doing. All of this could be added up and synthesized into a reasonably coherent whole called the "United States National Interest," at least as of that year. For a time that worked as an inductive method of defining national interest. But I am no longer confident that such a descriptive list would be ac cepted by even a majority of Americans as enabling them to inf a valid statement of American interests and national purpose the period ahead.

How does one get away from the Bismarckian view tha

tional interests are self-evident? or Napoleon's definition of national interest as the geography of one's country? Given these two, the whole thing is self-explanatory, and all policies are logical extensions of self-evident national interest. But clearly this combination of Bismarck and Napoleon, taken straight, has served our country increasingly badly. On the other hand, pure Woodrow Wilson, undiluted, has proven equally injurious to national health.

Some Americans—including Presidents—talk as though American national interests were immutable. But of course, apart from sheer survival, they are not. We may have preferences—a democratically-ruled, contented, admiring world around us—but we are forced to decide as a nation what is vital to us and what is not. To this extent attitudes, rather than geography or divine law, determine interests.

If Americans holding positions of power believe that the nature of the regime in South Vietnam—or Laos, or the Dominican Republic—is *vital* to the security of the United States—*and* such Americans are in a position to implement that belief and make it operational—it tends to *become* vital. This is a dynamic of the policy-making process in recent American experience. But there are few objective tests that such a process can survive. Hypothetically, if Israel disappeared from the map, presumably our oil supplies would be more secure, and what's more, the Russians would probably be kicked out of the Arab world in short order. What compelling interests of a strategic or economic nature is at stake in American support of Israel? Whether there may still be a "vital" interest is a point I want to answer later.

To take a second instance: if even after the sacrifices in Vietnam all Southeast Asia were to become a kind of Tonkinese Empire under Hanoi, neutralist at best or allied to China or Russia at worst, a reasonable argument may be made that it would not constitute a basic threat to any vital strategic balance, and that America's security, trade, and way of life would be fundamentally unaffected. Unless the domino theory or the Munich analogy can be more persuasively demonstrated, what *truly vital* U.S. security interest was really involved in the Vietnamese civil war? There is widespread agreement now that the answer is: *None.*

As a final example of recently undermined assumptions, it turns out that from the standpoint of vital security interests, a hostile Communist dictatorship ninety miles from America can be tolerated as easily as the Russians have tolerated hostile armed enemies on their borders all along (although unlike the Russians we have not tolerated nuclear missiles near ours). If one can live with this for decade after decade, then surely the definition of "vital" needs re-examination.

How can this be? Is nothing vital except our own survival as sentient human beings? I suspect that the answer to this is *Yes*—that nothing *is* vital except what is truly so, which is to say, affecting life itself. And so it must be, unless we want to let every corner of the world be defined by one or another politician or agency of government as "vital" and therefore deserving of a total American commitment. To make "vital" mean the same thing as "important" or "desirable" or "appropriate" (or possibly annoying or just interesting) not only degrades the language but may needlessly kill a lot of Americans. The semantics here involve not simply making words mean what you want them to mean, à la Lewis Carroll. Words may wind up changing the lives of people. "Vital interests" can refer only to the danger that the United States can be destroyed or mortally hurt. This may be the first element of clarity in sorting out what we have been calling "vital interests" all over the globe.

National interests cannot end with a geographical definition, however—at least not for the historic entity that is the United States. I have described our confusion between principles and pragmatism, and suggested that we have benefited neither from the quixotic ideal of a world in our image, nor from the practical actions we took in the name of an ideal—actions that in fact undermined its meaning. For surely one of the chief sources of the American malaise about foreign policy in recent years was that we often looked like unprincipled pragmatists in our own sphere, and pious moralists elsewhere. We need to return now to the tradition of an America that dealt realistically with the world while giving primacy to its democratic commitment *wherever its own writ ran*. This is not a return to isolationism any more than it is a prescription for renewed military interventionism. It is a step beyond both.

The Premises That Should Underlie Policy

What follows is my own "decalogue": ten assumptions that in my view *should* underlie U.S. policy, along with some illustrative actions that might implement needed changes in attitude. This is in no sense a comprehensive prescription for curing all policy ills. In the first place I am not qualified for that Herculean task. In the second, what I want to suggest here is broader dimensions of a policy attitude aimed at remedying the ills that I feel have most damaged us.

If anyone wants to call this a reinvigorated "liberal approach," he is welcome to. The important thing is not the ideological label, but the means—drawn from liberalism, conservatism, and even radicalism—that if applied to our problems might restore to Americans a fresh sense of national worth. My aim is to define in policy terms a general climate in which compassion and community are once again permitted to influence our policy calculations. The purpose is to bring some crucial policy sectors into better register with what is valid but has recently been missing in our self-portrait.

The dilemmas in doing what needs to be done are all too real, and I certainly cannot resolve them all. Nations must operate at a variety of levels; national goals, values and strategies have to be linked to the kind of world it really is. Nevertheless the most powerful nation, even while realistically limiting its attempts to manage the world, can by its actions and example still change the world by changing itself.

My decalogue comprises three kinds of premises. The first is the value premise that in a redefinition of national interest ought to override all others except actual survival.

1. *Neither states nor ideology nor things but people represent the highest value for American policy*

While men who are today in their fifties and sixties will continue to run this country for a few more years, many of those coming up behind them have an unusually strong sense that policy should rest on the conviction that the *human beings* who live in this country—and for that matter people everywhere—represent the irrefragably highest value for American policy: more than real estate, than investments, than virility, than strategic theory, than being Number One, even more than an abstract political or economic ideology, though all may have their place. This has to be the central point in a restatement of our ideology. It is linked to the spirit for which America used to stand. It is what many in the younger generation of Americans stand for. It can refurbish a tarnished image. Above all, it is ethically right.

The next three premises express the central realities in the external world—realities which we disregard at our peril but which, if focused on *exclusively*, drain U.S. foreign policy of its creativity.

2. *The balance-of-power mechanism still keeps the peace*

On the most fateful issues of national security the governing mechanism of world politics, so far as I can see, is still the balance of power. Events likely to upset the *overall* balance are perilous and should be resisted and corrected—although not by ourselves alone. By the same token, events that do not really upset the over-all balance should not be portrayed in terms of Munich, fighting on the beaches of California, or the Apocalypse. What is needed are policies that accept the central truth about the international system, but also actively search for more intelligent and acceptable strategies where vital balances are not threatened.

3. *Military power remains relevant to some—but by no means all—national strategies*

Blame for the recent U.S. obsession with military solutions primarily rests not on military men but on civilians who forgot that their business was diplomacy, conflict prevention, and compromise, and went chasing after shiny toys of power, subversion, and *force majeure*. The growing enormity of U.S. military power reinforced that tendency. Basic arms reduction is long overdue. But given the other realities, military power remains a crucially important element that is relevant to some (but by no means all) policy problems, such as deterrence of nuclear adventurism pending substantial arms reduction, and maintaining local balance of power along with serious efforts to settle outstanding conflicts.

4. *Hostile or incompatible forces remain in the world*

Only someone on a very powerful trip could fail to notice that the Cold War is not fully ended, that there still exist groups in the world, some ruling powerful countries, whose basic notions of how to organize and "improve" mankind are fundamentally different from ours, and that some of these leaders are deeply hostile to this country or, at a minimum, want what we have. In that connection I believe that how we ourselves change is going to affect this tension to some extent; in other cases it is not, and we had better maintain good intelligence and some dry powder. The existence of continent-pulverizing military strength in the hands of the second greatest industrial power in the world—the Soviet Union—makes that power not only the prime negotiating partner for the U.S. but also the prime adversary, as far as we can see ahead.

The Nixon Administration, even more than the two administrations before it, accepted this logic and deserves the thanks of all peace-inclined folk for its extraordinary efforts that yielded a first-step SALT agreement and increased trade relations, in addition to major outer space and scientific co-operation.

Three Presidents developed the habit of fairly close consultation that in the 1962 Cuban missile crisis helped keep things in hand, and did the same in the 1967 and 1973 Middle East wars and the 1971 India-Pakistan round. In the 1972 and 1973 Summit agreements both pledged mutual restraint, but Moscow urged additional Arab countries to join the 1973 Mid-East battle, and threatened unilateral military intervention. Obviously détente remains fragile and confrontations possible.

As I wrote earlier, I see the Soviets on two tracks, one messianic and trouble-making, the other détente-minded and pragmatic. No one can predict yet which will predominate. Substantial mutual arms reductions, accompanied by agreed verification procedures, may help break one link of the circular process of suspicion, fear, and hostility. A determined American program of measured unilateral steps may be effective, in the spirit of President Kennedy's American University speech.

Historical evidence is strong that feelings of community rest on common values, but are often strengthened by participating in common enterprises. In the U.S.—Soviet relation, common values are largely absent. But common interests abound, and U.S. policy should continue Mr. Nixon's excellent start and pursue such interests, particularly that of moving the basic quarrel to less expensive and dangerous means. This is not necessarily a theory of "convergence," but we can hope that common values will flow from shared experience.

A mixed relation must be expected to continue, and third parties are guaranteed to put strains on the relation. Fear of powerful partners conspiring against the weak was articulated by an Indian diplomat who spoke for many countries when he said, "If the Russians and the Americans are at loggerheads we are nervous, but when they get together we are terrified."

Since the appearance of such a conspiracy will be inevitable, the United States must work to dispel it, by a far more intimate relation with Europe and Japan. Above all, this country must never be tempted in a basic struggle for power to side with the Soviet Union against China, or vice versa; to do so could encourage precisely what must at all costs be avoided—the belief that nuclear aggression can be launched with relative impunity.

Paradoxically, the greatest tension in the decade ahead may arise from the inherent contradictions in Soviet policy in Eastern Europe. The détente Moscow seeks with the West implies increased East-West relations in Europe, which to Soviet alarm inevitably exposes Eastern Europe to the virus of liberalism and autonomy that Moscow proved unwilling to tolerate in Poland and Hungary in 1956, and Czechoslovakia in 1968. The fuse of détente may well end in Eastern Europe, making it perhaps the greatest potential area for large-scale violence and repression in the closing decades of this century. The dilemma for the West will be how to encourage better relations with Eastern Europe without encouraging uncontrollable developments that Moscow finds intolerable. The task for the intervening period is to begin to shape structures and relations that provide a framework for evolution but are not threatening to either West or East Europe. This is why the Conference on Security and Cooperation in Europe, instead of being feared by Washington as threatening NATO and the status quo, should have been seized on as opening the way at last to a long-term peaceful resolution of the division of Europe, while remaining strong in the process.

Outside Europe, both superpowers should negotiate to keep their fleets, their nuclear weapons, and their drive for predominant influence out of certain volatile regions not clearly within the ambit of either. One is Sub-Saharan Africa; another, North Africa; another, the Mediterranean islands; another, the Indian

Ocean; another, in time, Southeast Asia. This policy is the opposite of a deal on "spheres of influence" such as Britain and Russia negotiated over Persia in 1907 and over the Balkans in 1944. Such a policy can lead both to subjugation of peoples and, in our age, to tension between nuclear powers with the capacity to intervene. A good start was made in the 1972 and 1973 Summits in their discussions of mutual interest in avoiding collisions in third areas. It should logically be followed by negotiation to ensure that the eventual result is not spheres of interest but spheres of *abstention*. Otherwise history will repeat itself.

The remaining premises, and the policy actions related to them, go to the heart of my thesis. These are areas, problems, or situations where a basic change in the way the United States defines its interests and sets its priorities can help mightily to get us back on course.

5. *The United States has an influential world role, but no God-given mandate*

Jonathan Edwards' view of our celestial mandate is no longer applicable. We have no divine commission either to right all assumed wrongs or to impose our version of right or wrong on others, whether in their defense or not; nor does any other nation have that right. Near-omnipotence never did carry with it omniscience. The United States is still powerful enough to blow up the world, and almost rich enough to buy it. But somehow we haven't been proven to be wise enough to run it. So Good-bye (and, for my money, good riddance), Pax Americana.

At the same time, while the United States may not intervene unilaterally with military forces as before, its influence and power in the service of genuine war prevention, genuine collective security, and genuine humanitarianism will be desperately needed; as, in a few places, will its role as ally. Our role in Europe in the years ahead will test our capacity to free ourselves of stereotypes, and to act creatively yet responsibly in adapting to change. The United States has a deep and abiding interest—geographical, political, economic, and cultural—in a real partnership with as many European states as wish it. But the old partnership is obviously weakening, and hence U.S. objectives call for a creative effort to collaborate in the emerging design of a changed Europe.

One of the many tragedies of the Vietnam War was that it drained American creative powers in virtually every other sector of the world. Toward a Europe undergoing profound alterations in mood and in prospects, for all too long the best the United States was capable of was a sterile standpat-ism toward NATO, along with a jaded eye toward both Willy Brandt's *Ostpolitik* and the European Security and Cooperation Conference. Our lack of imagination has been compounded by our acceptance at face value the things European officials quite naturally say to discourage Americans from making any substantial troop withdrawals. The result has been a kind of laser effect, with European arguments bouncing back against U.S. repetition of the same reasoning, producing a self-paralyzing beam of possibly specious policy logic.

The thesis enunciated by Western Europeans and parroted by Americans had it that virtually any U.S. withdrawal would signal that the Soviet threat had disappeared and that the Western Europeans could forget their own security problems. Alternately, their demoralization would be so great that they would cut their own defensive dispositions and scramble to make their peace nation by nation with all-powerful Moscow, which would thus win its diabolical aim of a Europe consisting of broken and subservient "Finlands."

This thesis—expounded during the early 1970s by Americans occupying high positions of responsibility for these matters in Washington and at NATO headquarters—struck me as dangerously arrogant. It presumes that (a) Europeans do not understand their own interests; (b) Americans but not Europeans understand the Russians; and (c) Europeans are stupid. All three presumptions are unworthy of otherwise intelligent Americans (and Europeans who agree with them).

My own impression was that as West Europeans began to discount the inevitable reduction in American ground forces we were so careful to deny, a new impetus began to be felt for initiatives on the part of Western Europe to plan its own future. It was not a smooth process, particularly given French neo-Gaullism. Still, the admission of Britain and two other nations made the Common Market a potentially decisive confederation of nine; and the Davignon committee conducted quiet talks about the political and even security co-operation that could "spill over" from the new economic grouping.

Moreover, and in contrast to official American thinking, some Western Europeans, in and out of government, began to recognize that the chief hope of peace in Europe lay in grasping new opportunities to build it as a *whole*. A Conference on European Security and Cooperation, while it frightens those to whom any change is automatically "bad for us and good for the Russians," has set in train a process that may well last a decade or more. The outcome could be the creation of a web of structured relations among European nations of both East and West, within obvious but not necessarily immutable security limits and with the possibility of redressing the worst effects of the division of Europe. In fact the process is now inevitable, for good or not. While it is taking place, a firm U.S. military guarantee, plus a continued— though reduced—U.S. military presence in Western Europe will prevent Soviet miscalculation.

We of the United States are in a period of ambiguity. We cannot know how far Europe is able to go now toward détente, co-operation, and eventual unity between East and West. What we do know is that the frozen attitudes and policies of the 1950s and 1960s are inadequate to the vast changes even now altering the political face of Europe. As it was in 1947–49, so again in the

1970s there is thus a clear requirement for an intensive and courageous American reassessment of its relations with its oldest and closest partners—the Western European nations—in which the United States will help to fashion new structures of collaboration between equals, while accepting the growing independence of Europe's world role, along with genuine partnership in the crucial, interdependent sectors of trade, monetary policy, and energy. Common defense policies are not a reward for such partnership but protect our security as well as Europe's.

6. *The risk of nuclear war cannot be tolerated indefinitely*

However comfortably strategic analysts—and indeed almost everyone—have learned to live with nuclear weapons, if ever used they can still destroy civilization as we know it. Any responsible person who does not remain permanently alarmed about this seems to me to have lost his touch with both reality and humanity. Prevention of a nuclear war is the only policy goal directly related to the survival of the American (and all) people; by any definition of "vital" it belongs at the undisputed forefront of policy, strategy, and diplomacy. To act on this truth, two basic strategies deserve the highest American priority, one no less than the other, if the nuclear peace is to be kept: (1) maintenance of deterrence to major aggression; and (2) reversal of the strategic arms race.

For all their occasional indifference to human factors in implementing national security policies, the American centrist Establishmentarians who were in charge of those policies understood better than anyone else (the peace movement included) that World War III could be prevented only by making it continuously clear to a probing, thrusting, and messianic Soviet Union that, unlike the soft democracies of the 1930s, the post-war United States of America would not fail to retaliate against any Soviet armed aggression.

When that ceased to be the main worry, strategic deterrence often became confused with maintenance of U.S. nuclear "superiority," with being Number One in the world, and with the prosperity of the defense industry. As Soviet missile capabilities grew, Europeans came to understand that the United States was unlikely to sacrifice its own cities for European ones. Moreover, the likelihood of unprovoked direct Soviet military action against the West became minimal, if indeed it had ever been a possibility—whether thanks to successful Western deterrence we shall probably never know, at least not until the Kremlin opens its archives.

But for all that, the nuclear arsenals remained and, given a new crisis or change of leadership, the threat of a nuclear confrontation is always there. Until the world has a universal collective security system that works, deterrence of Soviet use of nuclear weapons remains an American responsibility (and vice versa). The formula remains unchanged, however bored with it people may become: to make clear that no surprise first strike can possibly succeed in wiping out the retaliatory capacity, which in turn is guaranteed to destroy the one who first drew the nuclear sword.

This is the reason the ABM development was so inherently dangerous, tempting as it was to be "defended." An expensive, "good" defense against incoming missiles just might prompt a ruthless (but sane) leader to believe that he could get away with launching his own missiles without being destroyed in return. It is almost irrelevant to speculate as to whether he would or would not: what really matters is that he might even *think* he would get away with it—with genocidal results. The essence of war prevention in the nuclear era is to prevent any such leader from thinking that way.

This in turn explains why all the early-warning intelligence and reassurance apparatus, however neurotic it makes both Russians and Americans seem about each other, is essential to give each the feeling that it cannot be wiped out before it is able to retaliate. A prime absurdity of the nuclear arms race is that actually one does not even need real weapons to deter, only the *belief* on the part of another that one has such weapons. If the secret could be kept, plywood or plastic missiles would do the deterrent job and save us a fortune, particularly since actually firing ICBM's would be the ultimate absurdity.

This is finally the reason nuclear "superiority" is dangerous nonsense. "Sufficiency" should be interpreted as sufficient not to "win a war"—which has become impossible—but to do what deterrence aims to do: i.e., convince the other side that whatever it does, it would be intolerably punished in return. Logically, this should mean drastic reduction in numbers, but this proves to be the hardest thing of all to do. (Just for mind-opening purposes I suggested to two successive heads of the U.S. Arms Control Agency, with no evident results, the parlor exercise of figuring out just what kind and what size of strategic forces we would need to do that job today *if we were starting from scratch.* It would be small.)

The first SALT agreements were thus only a first stage—the application of brakes. For within SALT I's agreed levels, sufficient weapons remained in national arsenals to destroy virtually all civilized life in the northern hemisphere (which is where nuclear weapons would be used). We have grown used to having the equivalent of fifteen tons of TNT under every bed in the world, just the way our ancestors became used to the possibility that the plague would strike. We have adapted in the sense that we have arranged to live our lives without the chronic panic most humans felt during the early nuclear years. But in the sense that a tiny number of fallible individuals—in the case of the United States only one—have only to give a command to put us all back in prehistory, the situation is wholly irrational and, over any long run, intolerable.

To the extent it makes actual cutbacks, SALT I's successor agreement will be even tougher to negotiate. Some still like to feel "superior," even though each new spiral of the nuclear arms race creates greater insecurity—a fact recognized by two of the hardest-headed administrations in the world at the time they negotiated SALT I. We can expect a bitter debate in both countries if it comes to reductions. Still, on rational grounds there is only one real question: What must you have in order to continue to persuade the other that it would be suicidal to use or even threaten to launch his nuclear weapons?

The human obstacles to a rational solution to the nuclear arms race are four. First come the "hard-nosed" on both sides who consider thermonuclear weapons different from conventional weapons in degree only, and believe that a nuclear war can be "won" (however insane the reasoning). Second are the political fanatics around the world who, in the name of their particular cause, seem blithely prepared to take risks of war involving nuclear powers—which is why at almost all cost the Nuclear Non-Proliferation Treaty must be maintained. Third are those well-meaning but soft-headed utopians who for years have monopolized the movements for "peace and disarmament" with unrealizable schemes, thus retarding efforts to mobilize popular understanding and to pressure governments to take bold but realizable steps toward a solution. In this sense the disarmers have given disarmament a bad name, which is unfortunate, given the importance of the problem.

Fourth are the sincere (and influential) people on both sides who worry about technological breakthrough and cheating on agreements by one or the other side, and also fear that cutting down the redundancy of nuclear systems will somehow make it easier for the other side to do things with impunity—other than launching war—which presumably it can't do now. After listening very hard to this group, I remain unconvinced. For they cannot tell me what specific things nuclear weapons inhibited in the past, that they would expect the Soviets to *do* in future when we might have only half the number of launchers than at present; nor can they specify what *we* would *not* be able to do with greatly reduced nuclear stockpiles and inventories, that we have been able to do freely up to now.

The reason they cannot make these lists is that the argument is false. In actual fact, possessing quantities of nuclear weapons reduces rather than increases a nation's freedom of action, makes it more cautious, has little or no effect on the secondary or peripheral mischief that other nations make, and certainly does not deter revolutions, invasions by third nations, hate propaganda, anti-Americanism (or anti-Sovietism), trade and currency conflicts, or anything except that for which it continues to be useful—namely, a deliberate attack by a superpower threatening the security of the other or its closest allies. As a senior Soviet expert commented ironically to me in a meeting in Moscow in the spring of 1973, analysis has shown them that increases in both U.S. and Soviet military strength are more and more accompanied by decreases in their influence.

A detailed analysis of this problem was made by the U.S. Department of Defense under Secretary McNamara, and its validity has never been persuasively challenged. The gist of the analysis (publicized only that one time) was that even with anti-ballistic missiles, four hundred or so deliverable strategic warheads would inflict intolerable damage on the Soviet Union, destroying 30 per cent of the people and three-fourths of industrial capacity (Secretary of Defense, Defense Program, and 1969 Defense Budget, p. 57). What we know of the actual thinking of both Soviet and American leaders has seemed to support McGeorge Bundy's conclusion that even one city lost is likely to be too much for any sane leader to accept. We now have more than ten times four hundred strategic warheads in our inventory (in addition to thousands of tactical warheads, some of which look very strategic indeed to people whose homeland they can destroy). A single one of our converted Poseidon-firing submarines can now launch enough nuclear warheads to do as much as one-third the entire job of destruction. Yet arguments continue for vast new strategic delivery system programs.

The goal should be an agreement reducing the present inventory of thousands of strategic nuclear warheads on both sides to a number much smaller but still capable of delivering four hundred (or even two hundred) nuclear warheads on the vital centers of the would-be aggressor, no matter how he struck first. This means that with the present U.S. submarine fleet alone, and not even counting our vast land-based missile arsenal or our scores of heavy bombers, we could continue to do the one thing that deterrence requires. There is no evidence that it will be possible to track submarines during the 1970s in such a way as to nullify this massive deterrent force.

The inescapable conclusion from this line of reasoning is that the United States can and should start thinking big and bold (instead of small and nervous) about turning the nuclear arms race around. If there were no nuclear weapons we would surely all agree that if any nation had to have them the rational limit would be something less than one hundred—say, fifty: enough to incapacitate both societies for years. Instead, inured by decades of stockpiling, we are stuck with thousands, all unusable—or, if used—suicidal.

If Russia and the United States have to keep some atomic weapons as a deterrent—which they do in this era of continued although abating political warfare and military risk—then our target should be a number that corresponds not to what we have but to what is needed. The process is helped by the growing obsolescence of fixed land-based missiles, which, given both U.S. and Soviet MIRV's, will in a few years all be vulnerable to salvo attacks. The sensible thing is to work toward total elimination of fixed land-based missiles while reaching an agreement on missile test-firings to control any further development of MIRV; toward limits on anti-submarine warfare, in order to enable the invulnerable deterrent to survive and thus spare us costly new arms races; and perhaps toward something as far-reaching as joint guarantees to any nation that deliberately disarms, in order to encourage breakthroughs in the dismal cycles of action and reaction the world over. If we need a motto that appeals to the emotions while accurately describing the situation, I would offer "Mutual Superiority."

Finally, the Americans and the Russians ought to stop evading the question—which they have for years—and act to ban underground nuclear tests, so as to close the loop on the test-ban treaty. Thus they could demonstrate both their will to turn the arms race around and their sensitivity to the charges of hypocrisy from the more than a hundred nations we are asking to renounce the nuclear game altogether.

7. *Worldwide strivings for economic, social, and racial equality will intensify, creating new instabilities*

All projections into the future confirm the cynical proposition that "The rich get richer and the poor get children." The Gross National Product gap will combine with racism to create a built-in source of tension. It may be true that, as historian Carl Becker once observed, "Nothing is inevitable until after it has happened." But one doesn't have to be either a Marxist or a fortune-teller to see that, on the basis of our experience so far, we can forecast an increasing pace of uprisings on the part of the poor, the oppressed, and the discriminated-against. On a scale of probability and imminence, led by Latin Americans and trailed by central Africans, this tension will persist until the deprived ones gain a greater measure of equality with rich, white, Western man.

A constructive American approach to the Third World runs the risk of being insufficient and even trivial unless a revised philosophy underlies our modified policies. Such a philosophy should be based on two principles: a more relaxed U.S. stance toward seeming "instability" in the Third World, a stance involving acceptance in volatile and growing societies of the inevitability of change, sometimes revolutionary, sometimes violent; and a new commitment to give primacy to political, social, and economic justice, where that is the issue.

THE LIGHT AT THE END OF THE TUNNEL

The notion of revolution presents a complex problem for Americans, since *we* think approvingly of political revolutions such as those in 1688 and 1776, while *others* think of societal and structural revolutions as in 1789, 1848, 1917, and 1949. This confusion increases the potential error in a policy resting chiefly on an attachment to stability. If the United States, in pursuit of stability, lets that mean any kind of governmental rule so long as there is no international war or domestic violence, this nation is likely to find itself underwriting, or in any event tolerating, conditions that in the longer run produce precisely that which it most fears—revolution, anti-Americanism, and possibly Communism. The error is not in the interest in stability. It is in disregarding both the logic and the lessons of history on how to gain peace with justice through "dynamic stability."

Giving the dependent or the genuinely disaffected a piece of the action, a stake in the community, transforming their alienation to constructive participation, seems to me the only proven way to stability. Put differently: repression is often immoral, and usually unsuccessful (unless one runs a ruthless totalitarian state). On the other hand—and this is what the "realists" never seem to learn—justice pays. It is ignorance more than malevolence that motivates otherwise moral Americans to pursue immoral foreign policies.

This is not merely an abstraction. Let me return to the American interest in Israel. The Jewish community in Palestine was one of the most unstable elements on the world scene when it was fighting the British in the 1940s. Israel today is a stable, democratic state. The region is still unstable, largely because not all of Israel's neighbors accepted that state's right to exist. Until they do, and until it is recognized by all (including Israel) that the same right is due the Arab Palestinians, there will be no true stability.

India today is a status-quo power. Nothing so annoyed the British during World War II as American support for post-war independence for India. But irritated as Winston Churchill was, Britain remained our faithful ally, and the United States had at least some part in averting a bloody colonial war between Britain and India—undoubtedly one of the greatest favors we ever did our ally. What if we had similarly followed our historical instincts in French Indochina in May of 1950, when the issue was still predominantly one of independence from a colonial ruler—France? What if, instead of telling Cambodian Prince Sihanouk—as Secretary Dulles did in 1953—to thank God he had the French (Sihanouk interview with Oriana Fallaci, *New York Times Magazine*, August 12, 1973, p. 15), we had followed President Roosevelt's avowed policy and encouraged local autonomy and development? How many dead Americans, and Vietnamese, would still be alive? Years later in an interview Dean Acheson had the grace to acknowledge that we had acted contrary to our interests because France had "blackmailed" us (*New York Times Book Review*, October 12, 1969, p. 30).

The net effect of elevating undifferentiated stability to paramount place in American policy toward the Third World had the perverse effect of putting this nation on the wrong side of certain issues that many Americans feel are fundamental to their own history and ideology. Thucydides once remarked that there are always people, like the Athenians of his day, who are "born into the world to take no rest themselves and to give none to others." The question for the United States is whether it is to be permanently cast as the enemy of all new movements, tendencies, and historical forces. For that seems to me the trap we have set for ourselves.

Nothing in the U.S. Constitution says we have to be allies of small-time dictatorships, one-party police states, and unpopular oligarchies, *unless* we are in a war in which our very existence is at stake. Nor do I see anything that says we have to be fundamentally hostile to regimes that call themselves "socialist." Isn't it really time that as a people we learned that both at home and abroad today's instability may be the only way to acquiring a stake in the established order and coming into the community as a fruitful contributor?

As for my second prescription—a renewed U.S. commitment to values of political democracy and economic and social justice—it may be argued that our recent troubles have stemmed precisely from an attempt to impose our own values on unwilling or ungrateful recipients. In Indochina, looking not at the ruling elites but at the people, more than one American has asked, "With allies like us, who needs enemies?" How can I propose what might seem like a new Wilsonian globalism, entailing interventionism with a vengeance, just when we have begun to back away from automatic interventionist policies?

The answer is that I am not. What is needed is a policy that *discriminates* between different classes of situations and states (just as, in a way, the vague Nixon Doctrine does). *Category No. 1* includes situations in which we cannot impose our values, have no particular right to, might produce World War III if we tried to, and yet must work hard toward better relations. Here is where pragmatism and an ideology-free policy are required, and here is where the Nixon-Kissinger *Realpolitik* went a good distance toward de-ideologizing our vitally important state-to-state relations with the Soviet Union and China, placing them instead on a desirable "business-like" basis, as the Soviets like to put it. This rescued U.S. policy from the Wilson-Dulles trap of futile and self-deluding crusades, and could fruitfully be applied today to Cuba.

The *second category* includes those places in the world that we have consciously and deliberately identified as crucial American interests, and where we have proceeded to create dependent client states which we support with U.S. taxpayers' funds—in many cases even down to their day-to-day budgets. Such has been the case in recent years, for good reasons and bad, in Taiwan, South Korea, South Vietnam, Thailand, Laos, Cambodia, Greece, Turkey, Pakistan, and in varying measure in other countries both in the so-called advance base areas of Asia, and in the "northern tier" of the Middle East.

It is situations such as these, where we actually influence events or where we entrust client states and allies with our own reputation, that the United States must become far more sensitive to values of democracy and social and economic justice. The arguments *pro* and *con* on this issue have raged for years. There is now ample evidence that on balance our national interests suffer when we take responsibility for virtually running another country in order to preserve its "freedom of choice," but then look on helplessly while it represses its own people, corrupts itself with our wealth, and turns the American people cynical and embittered.

In the rest of the world the Nixon-Kissinger strategy correctly pursued a foreign policy that was substantially less doctrinaire than its predecessors. I am arguing also, however, that the policy seemed to me to err gravely in applying the same "value-free" *Realpolitik* to the *rest* of American foreign policy, swallowing one-man elections in South Vietnam, choosing the undemocratic side in the India-Pakistan relation, encouraging the Greek colonels in their most repressive period of rule to believe they had our full support, and further downgrading both the humanitarian and multilateral aspects of American diplomacy in every way except verbally.

This foregoing reference brings me to a *third category* of external problems to which the United States should apply the lessons of Vietnam and generally of unilateral interventionism. These involve the areas, chiefly in the Third World, in which no substantial U.S. interest exists but where we have tried, often inappropriately, to impose American values while seeking often non-existent strategic advantage. If neo-isolationism means anything constructive, it means to decouple U.S. policy from direct involvement in such areas for either ideological or strategic gain, and instead to refocus policy on humanitarian concern for welfare, along with multilateral institution-building and problem-solving.

THE LIGHT AT THE END OF THE TUNNEL

The so-called Nixon Doctrine sought to decouple direct U.S. military power from this last group of states, but gave primary emphasis to the furnishing of military assistance. To get at the deeper roots of the problem, I would urge that this third grouping, which represents the great majority of peoples and of states in the world, ought to be approached by the United States with a set of new policies that reflect more faithfully our commitment to preventing conflict, and to the building of a better world order in acts rather than in words.

On the positive side of the ledger we face the stark fact of American superwealth *versus* superpoverty in the developing countries, a gap predicted to grow. The United States with about 6 per cent of the world's population consumes annually about 30 per cent of its available resources and services. A more equitable distribution of this wealth lies at the core of the global debate about North-South relations. Yet as the mid-1970s approached, the U.S. foreign economic assistance program was a disaster area, with little or no Congressional or popular support and a decline in giving to about one-quarter of 1 per cent (.0025) of the GNP —which puts us about fifteenth among contributing nations on the basis of GNP percentage—this from the richest nation in human history.

Virtually all the arguments for a "generous program" of redistribution through aid, preferential loans, and the like have fallen to the ground. What remains is the least pragmatic—but perhaps the most powerful—argument of all: that the United States cannot really fulfill its primary national purpose of living a fruitful and fulfilling life as a nation or as an aggregate of individual citizens simply as a bastion fortified against the miseries and poverty of others—an armed suburb, so to speak, outside which the city rages. The only viable motive for generous aid to poor nations is humanitarianism, with the same spiritual and psychic benefits to the donor that the individual enjoys when he gives to the poor in his community.

Unrealistic? Not if the United States wishes to recapture the sense of feeling *good* about itself which it experienced with such high points in American—and world—history as Herbert Hoover's European relief efforts after World War I, the outpouring of U.S. aid to Japan after the 1923 earthquake, Lend-Lease, the Marshall Plan, Truman's Point Four Technical Assistance program, and other occasions when American wealth and power were expressed in giving.

8. *International conflicts are likely to continue, and some of them will endanger a wider peace*

Despite their logic, the forces that make for solutions—such as better world order, substantial armament reduction, and more equitable distribution of the world's goods—seem weaker than ever before. Meanwhile, the forces that make for conflict, such as virulent nationalism, are increasing in Africa, Asia, and Eastern Europe, and in pockets within the allegedly advanced Northern countries. Our local conflict study at M.I.T. counts sixty military-type conflicts since World War II. Over 90 per cent have taken place not in Europe but in the developing regions. Less than 50 per cent of the "insurgencies" among those sixty conflicts have been primarily Communist in provenance. There is nothing to indicate that the present rate of about 1.5 new conflicts per year will not continue and even increase, considering the roster of unresolved quarrels, old colonialism, new imperialism, collapse of new countries, liberation movements (including those within Socialistic countries), and ethnic, religious, linguistic, and racial conflict in developed societies. At the mid-1970s, half the nations of the world—about seventy—were either engaged in conflict or actively preparing for conflict.

The lesson of recent history is that if we want to prevent wars —and I believe we do—we have to do far more than try to stop the shooting after it starts. The India-Pakistan War of 1971 was simply another demonstration that U.S. policy toward local conflicts in the developing regions still limits itself to traditional diplomacy when conflict builds, and overreacts when the conflict finally explodes into violence. Wholly apart from the unwisdom of Mr. Nixon's preference for Pakistan in that war, this is a chronic problem with deep roots in the American style of policy-making. Until it is squarely faced, there will be no success for diplomacy and no end to dangerous violence abroad.

If in 1971 the United States had had a *sound* policy for control of conflict, it would have concentrated its pre-hostilities efforts on the central substantive issues of self-determination and refugees, accepting the high diplomatic cost, which might have been no higher than helping make India an open Soviet ally. If we had had a *principled* foreign policy, it would have rested on the democratically-expressed will of the great majority of East Pakistanis, and focused our enormous influence to prevent that popular will from being savagely frustrated, as in fact it was. Instead, "friendship" with the dictatorial and inept General Yahya Khan came first, while polite efforts were made to persuade. But we know now that the price of "not annoying Yahya," of "not rocking the boat," of "keeping open our lines of communication," "using quiet diplomacy," "not jeopardizing our influence," and all the other customary formulas, was excessive. In the end there was no more united Pakistan and no more Yahya Khan. Meanwhile the United States was once again censured in much of the world and at home for seeming to betray its own ideals concerning human rights and the right of people freely to determine their own future, a right for which over forty thousand American lives had already been sacrificed in Vietnam.

Our "don't annoy Yahya" posture reportedly bought us a secure channel for the approach of China. But other channels were open none of them requiring support for a barbarous and dictatorial ally. In any event, it proved to be pragmatically shortsighted.

When in his Second Inaugural Address President Nixon said

that "the time has passed when America will make every other nation's conflict our own," he was correctly reflecting the lessons of the times. But those conflicts can still hurt us and hurt world peace. There is still a high vocation in the role of peacemaker; and the United States, despite everything, has much to give to that task. Thus it is that we can derive further lessons from the India-Pakistan conflict of 1971 and the fourth-round Middle East war of 1973. What should influential outside states have done in the Middle East, before fighting broke out again, that we learned by failure to do in East Pakistan at a comparable stage?

The lesson is that in the Middle East the U.S. should have focused on the basic *causes* of the chronic war there, accepting the short-term diplomatic costs. The primary cause is the lack of a self-determined homeland for the Palestinian Arabs, just as perpetual war with the British Mandatory Power was ensured until that same right was granted to the Jewish people. That not having been faced, another bloody round of warfare was virtually guaranteed.

The only way to break the endless chain of error and failure is through a better learning process that gets built into both attitudes and process. The primer could well be the sensible things Henry Kissinger said, when he was first appointed to advise Mr. Nixon, about finding the time and perspective to get ahead of crises instead of lurching from one to the next.

One is reminded once again that the downgrading of long-range policy planning as a valued function is one error that should be corrected. But beyond that must be a deep conviction on the part of the President and his advisers that it is not enough to be crisis managers if we wish to affect the dismal cycle of inevitable conflict. American diplomacy is at its most shallow, not to say hypocritical, when it contends that the only real sin is national military forces crossing another nation's borders. Press Secretary Ziegler said with indignation in December 1971, "The way to stop war is not to turn up the tanks and fill the guns with bullets." Of course war is an evil disease; but it cannot be seriously treated with Band-aids. Mr. Ziegler articulated precisely the misconception that is guaranteed to keep us several steps behind in the most dangerous game in the world.

9. *The major forces affecting human life on the planet are increasingly trans-national and require purposeful steps toward world order*

The things that affect human life at the human level are what it is really all about, despite the chronic delusion of bureaucracies the world over that society exists to support them and their programs. The greatest single lesson for leadership, and the heart of the needed transformation in American attitudes about its world role, turns on this point: Nation-states will continue to act as though sovereignty were total; but the air, the water, the food sources, the quality of people's lives, the communications that enrich them, the wars and diseases that kill them, the consequences of affluence and of scientific discovery—every single one of these will turn out upon analysis to be largely indifferent to a single nation's boundaries and effectively approachable only on the basis of regional or international co-operation and ultimately of international regulation.

Even if we and other peoples are not ready for this insight, it is nevertheless a towering fact—as is the fact that only states can undertake the diplomacy essential for solving these problems. It follows that the development of genuinely effective multilateral instruments and agencies has become for the first time in history a sheer necessity instead of a luxury.

The U.N. Conference on the Environment held in Stockholm in 1972 marked a splendid start, and one that should be followed up on global and regional levels if the international community is to move decisively toward effective international standards and controls. Within a few years communications satellites will be able to broadcast directly into receivers at home. An international

FCC with real regulatory powers will be needed so that this revolutionary communications potential will not become a cockpit for war and hate propaganda (or for deodorant commercials on a global scale.) Population growth, which continues to wipe out both economic growth plans and the hope of mortals in crowded countries for a decent life, requires many times the international effort now being put into it.

We must elevate to a far higher plane of policy the design of effective strategies for international control of outer space, and equivalent controls to ensure the equitable exploitation of the riches of the seabed and its subsoil to avert the inevitable scramble for power and the conflicts bred of greed that have characterized all previous frontier-opening enterprises. Both require nothing short of international regulatory agencies with genuine powers, and it should be U.S. policy to achieve such a goal.

There are still other problem areas where the traditional nationalistic political and strategic thinking reigns supreme but where only a change in that frame of mind can avoid unwanted conflicts. A case in point is the issue of vital international straits and waterways. The list is short but enormously significant; and while each among them is under the control of a single state, practically all are contested by one or more competitors.

No more vivid example can be found for the contradictory and potentially self-defeating thinking of traditionalists than that of the Suez Canal. France and Britain conspired with Israel in 1956 to launch a surprise attack on Egypt in retaliation for having expropriated the Canal. During the fateful summer preceding the war there seemed a chance that Egypt might agree to adjudication of the dispute by the International Court of Justice.

U.S. Secretary of State Dulles, who preached the rule of law in public, in private discouraged any such sensible and peaceful step on the ground that it might legally jeopardize the U.S. position in Panama. The bloody and futile military adventure that followed validated the Egyptian seizure, ended England's pretensions to extended great-power status, confirmed to the great majority of nations their beliefs about unreconstructed Western imperialism—and of course made it impossible to confront with clean hands the simultaneous and equally bloody Soviet repression of the Hungarian quest for political freedom.

Without enumerating here the details of the mounting crisis the U.S. faces in maintaining its quasi-sovereign status in the middle of the State of Panama, it is enough to observe that all the discussion on both sides of the issue has been framed basically in terms of competitive American and Panamanian sovereignty. As nationalism mounts in Panama, and overseas extraterritorial rights become repudiated—as they increasingly have been and will be, the conditions for a replay of the Suez tragedy are created. There is no discussion whatever of a third status—i.e., neither total U.S. control nor total Panamanian control of a waterway vital to many countries, but an international status ensuring three conditions: 1) the unimpaired self-respect of Panama; 2) uninterrupted access to the Canal regardless of fluctuating U.S.-Panamanian relations; and 3) responsible involvement of the international community in this (and other) waterways representing jugular veins on which the planet as a whole depends.

Three other straits are of comparable (if not greater) strategic significance, where violent conflict has either taken place, or is predictable precisely because the straits are narrow, vulnerable, and yet vital to the life of other countries.

The flash point for the June 1967 war between Egypt and Israel was the same narrrow Strait of Tiran, at the mouth of the Gulf of Aqaba, which had similarly triggered the 1956 Suez War. When Egypt closed the Strait in May 1967, the options other than war shrank perilously—as they invariably will when one nation can sever another's jugular.

The Turkish Straits represent a vital egress for the Soviet Union, Bulgaria, and Rumania. Some international agreements were worked out—the 1923 Treaty of Lausanne, modified at

Montreux in 1936—ensuring such access. But more than once in the early post-war years a suspicious and hostile Russia threatened to take the Straits by force. In the case of Suez a comparable treaty (the Constantinople Convention of 1888) was no guarantee of peace when relations had otherwise deteriorated.

The Strait of Hormuz is unfamiliar to most Americans, but will probably not be so for long; it has become intimately familiar to Western Europeans and the Japanese, which depend on the Persian Gulf for over 80 per cent of their vital petroleum needs. The islands commanding the mouth of the Gulf (Abu Musa, Greater Tunb, and Lesser Tunb) have already been seized by Iran (which is acquiring, chiefly from the United States, about $3 billion worth of sophisticated new weaponry). The Japanese lifeline passes also through the long and narrow Strait of Malacca between Singapore, Malaysia, and Indonesia.

The list is longer than that. But the point ought to be clear. Extant are many proposals spelling out the details of international régimes for such waterways, including one advanced by President Truman at Potsdam in 1945 but never renewed by the U.S. Government since. Once the principle is accepted, it would not be beyond the wit of men to design a régime short of international ownership but a step beyond the animal-kingdom-type "territorial imperative" that dominates such thinking as is focused on this subject. The time is not unlimited, as the twelve-mile limit becomes generally accepted, wiping out existing unrestricted high-seas lanes and requiring new rules on free passage.

On the *peace-keeping* front, the turn once again in desperation to the United Nations in the Middle East war of 1973 proves the need to design strengthened international capabilities to avoid nuclear superpower intervention in local conflicts. Yet in recent years both superpowers, far from drawing this conclusion, acted to weaken the fragile instrument that is the United Nations. Avoiding all serious use of the United Nations in Vietnam was only one case in point.

The chief danger is not that the United Nations will die, but that it will settle into a condition of permanent invalidism. The heart of the problem is not that the United States and other major powers ignore the United Nations; it is that their short-run view of what will advance their individual national interests positively excludes the United Nations from a serious place in matters of moment. Their estimates of the likely headaches involved in U.N. action are all too accurate. The trouble is that their longer-range interests in a more predictable and just world order require that they run more short-term risks and pay more short-term costs—and that is precisely what they are unwilling to do.

It has comforted some Americans to believe that the United Nations' decline was chiefly the fault of the Soviet Union. At one time I believed that this was so. But increasingly the United States, while giving lip-service to multilateralism, has itself acted unilaterally, often in disregard of majority opinions. This policy has been thoroughly bipartisan. While arguing that the United Nations was unable to handle vital questions, we have given it fewer important things to do. The effect is to create a self-fulfilling prophecy, to produce a United Nations increasingly incapable of dealing with anything very important.

In recent years the United States has increasingly acted the role of the biggest boy in the club sulking when others take center stage, occasionally himself wrecking a piece of the clubhouse, and then turning around and saying "You see, this place is no good." Example? U.N. sanctions, voted by an overwhelming majority including the United States against the breakaway white-minority régime in Rhodesia that dominates and keeps in a humiliatingly inferior status its great majority population of five million blacks. Who broke the U.N. embargo on imports from Rhodesia? The United States, that's who. And then we say, "You see, the UN is ineffective."

Example? In 1971 President Nixon decided to change the

twenty-year policy of American opposition to the entry of Communist China into the United Nations. He did not do so on the ground of universality, which would have admitted all the divided states and thus would have made the best possible argument for keeping Taiwan in. He also knew that Peking's condition for coming in was the ouster of Taiwan. By his strategy he turned what should have been a victory for common sense into an all-out fight it was impossible to win.

When Peking was admitted—as we wanted, and Taiwan expelled—which we did not want but made inevitable by our tactics, some foreign representatives did not hesitate to vent their glee over the final collapse of a widely unpopular U.S. policy. There ensued a display of U.S. pique and malice toward the United Nations which sought to deflect from the White House the rage of the American right wing by dumping the blame on the United Nations, along with dire threats and self-fulfilling prophecies. I had a personal reason for distress at this display of destructive behavior for the sake of quick domestic tricks, for as a member of the President's Commission to advise him on the future of the United Nations I had found myself the one to urge that the United States put itself in an advantageous and defensible position in the United Nations for the first time in years by adopting a principle that would commend itself widely to others, the principle of total universality.

But it is not just the President. Any President makes big calculations and is likely to decide that the United Nations is expendable compared with some short-term political or strategic objective of his own. The problem goes deep into the bureaucracy of government, too—and I mean the government of almost all major nations. In the United States I have observed over the years that even when the United Nations is showing signs of succeeding in some area, a pervasive cynicism exists within government. Where anything crucially important to U.S. interest is concerned, the United Nations is generally the last place U.S. decision-makers will turn. Confronted with proposals to strengthen the United Nations or to multilateralize one or another matter, the most dedicated and high-minded government official is still likely to react almost instinctively to minimize any constraints that might be imposed on total American freedom of action. (The parallel vis-à-vis the Congress is striking). Many other governments reason identically.

All this reflects something even more fundamental, in what might be called the "foreign policy culture." Typically, a proposal to take a hard line, or narrow view of U.S. interests, is more often than not deemed "realistic," while advocating compromise or partnership brands one as "soft." Why waste one's time therefore with a line of policy reasoning that is hard to implement, runs counter to short-term trends, and exposes one to the ridicule reserved for the "unrealistic"?

The answer is quite clear to me. It is that the hard-headed, unilateral, close-to-the-chest, keep-all-your-options-open approach of the "realist" is increasingly out of keeping with the nature of the external problem this nation faces. The truly hard-nosed advice may well be that which recommends interpreting the national interest far more broadly—that is, by taking bold moves to pool authority and giving a new lead to co-operative rather than unilateral directions.

Where do we go from here? Let us concede without equivocation that the United Nations is a pretty ineffective, inefficient, and even unmanageable instrument for doing quite a number of things that need doing. But let us accept another premise: that the United States is decreasingly likely to intervene unilaterally outside of a few genuinely vital areas, and thus a multilateral substitute may become a sheer necessity rather than a luxury; and the further premise that some of our own rhetoric about the need for an improved world order is persuasive and deserves to be converted from myth to reality. Where would we begin to try to stem the tide of rot and to reverse the dismal direction of events? In an article (*New York Times*, July 21, 1971) I suggested for mind-stretching purposes a couple of admittedly far-out proposals.

a. The chances for any basic improvements in world order now depend on the consent of the lowest common denominator. Rather than waiting for Communists to become capitalists, or the poor nations to become rich, the United States should organize *coalitions* within the United Nations of those who are willing now to accept certain recommendations of specified majorities on questions of genuine importance to the nations concerned. In other words, to create *fragments of community*, so to speak, with shifting groups of those who share basic values and premises on a certain issue and are willing to forego a degree of freedom of action thereon. Their shared values on the issue constitute elements that in any polity help to make up true community. We cannot have the community; but we can be seriously working toward building it by encouraging such "coalitions of the willing."

Such coalitions would agree in advance to take as binding certain unanimously agreed resolutions of U.N. bodies, or actions carried by majorities they would agree to in advance. One coalition of states interested in advancing the progress of international law might agree in advance and without reservation of any sort to be bound by the judgments of compulsory arbitration and adjudication, and to terms of settlement of disputes reached by the Security Council under Articles 37 and 38, in disputes involving two members of the coalition—but only with respect to other countries that have taken the same pledge. And so on.

b. The United States, correctly, is unwilling to accept as having binding force the judgments of a majority of members of the United Nations who might, in theory, represent only a fraction of the world's power or contributions to the U.N. budget. But a majority would probably never agree to have their power weakened by formal schemes of weighted voting. What I propose is that the United States unilaterally decide that it will accept as binding the judgments and recommendations of the General Assembly on important questions if, by a weighted scale, that vote represents a meaningful majority in terms of strength, population, power, or other criterion. No Charter change would be necessary. No other nation would have to change its policy. Our gamble would be that others might gradually come to see the common cause in our action, and the promise it holds of actually moving away from words toward a working world order.

Suggestions like these are merely provisional, designed to help tide us over a period in which not only the United Nations but all other institutions (including governments as presently organized) seem in many ways unresponsive to the needs of society, whether national or greater-than-national. Today the United Nations and the regional organizations do not come close to doing the job that needs doing, and their nibbling at the fringes simply will not be sufficient. It is now time to take a new look at the bone structure of international organization on the basis of almost a third of a century of experience, in order to determine what changes are needed. We should no longer hesitate to reopen the most fundamental premises and components of the U.N. Charter. It could hardly worsen the behavior of the member states, and it might help.

In the U.N. era one of the crowning ironies has been the increase in the use of force unilaterally to achieve a state's political ends. Nasser exercised it by seizing the Suez Canal Company in 1956, invading Yemen in 1962, and declaring a blockade of the Strait of Tiran in 1967. His successor attacked Israel in 1973. Britain, France, and Israel resorted to military attack on Egypt in 1956, and Israel did so again in 1967. India invaded East Pakistan in 1971 and even during her period of greatest international piety did not hesitate to do the same in Hyderabad in 1948 and Goa in 1961. China invaded Tibet, Indonesia attacked Malaysia, Ghana tried hard to subvert neighbors, and the list is endless.

The United States shares with the Soviet Union the dubious honor of demonstrating the will of the strongest nations to engage in international lawlessness by ignoring the fundamental bedrock injunction of the Charter to refrain from the unilateral use of force. Because it was able to get away with it, Russia invaded Hungary and Czechoslovakia and furnished the munitions to enable Hanoi and Cairo to seek their objectives by military means. But I cannot exculpate my own country from having unilaterally intervened without any international sanction or firm basis in international law in Lebanon in 1958 (on the heels of a U.N. observer group), the Bay of Pigs in 1961, the Dominican Republic in 1965, and Cambodia in 1970 (and before, in a major bombing campaign kept secret even from the Congress). Both powers had "good reasons" for what they did, and acted in their "higher national interest." But in none of these cases did they even consider applying the multilateral procedures they had devised.

Thus no one is blameless. But the great powers led the way. It is now open once again to the United States to show that a contrast exists between the cynical, power-oriented, imperialistic behavior of others, and the willingness of a democratic power like the United States to give primacy to other values such as peaceful change, political democracy, human rights, and social justice. That vision of a better world, backed by a humane and self-restrained outlook that avoids crusades but says what it thinks is right, is the first giant step back to being Number One not in arrogance but in decency.

The second step is to ascertain what, after a third of a century, has been learned about the prevention of war and the discouragement of aggression, and what agencies of the community, imperfect and split as it is, might constitute realistic beginnings of a true police power. In this spirit collective security (which was utopian for the late 1940s) deserves a serious new look. The same is true of U.N. peacekeeping, whose future role should be to try to insulate areas of conflict and change against outside interference. Whether recognized by its author or not, it seems an obvious corollary of the Nixon Doctrine. The motto for such a policy is "Change without Escalation."

With or without a revised set of institutions and rules, the practical challenge will be to act *despite* the lack of real community in the world as a whole, *despite* profound ideological differences, and *despite* the "balkanizing" trends and the tribalism that is rampant in all sectors. Proposals that require eliminating ideologies, ending tribalism, or reforming human nature are futile.

The most narrowly focused advantage-seeker frequently appeals in the same breath for something called "world order." Yet—and this is one of our chief problems—he keeps current policy carefully separated from that rhetorical goal, and never thinks to pay the price of possible short-term costs in order actually to stem the negative tide to which he contributes, and make a start toward construction of the better world order he claims to seek. For an American statesman such a tangible effort would conform to both the nation's self-image, and to the vision a great majority of Americans still hold of a better world.

It is not a lack of ideas about how to begin to make improvements in multilateral machinery that keeps the process from starting. It is a lack of vision and of political will. Both are curable defects.

10. *A policy is good not because it is ours but because it is right*

This is an aphorism—for which I apologize—and yet I believe Abraham Lincoln would have put it high on *his* policy "decalogue." It may in fact be the most important one of all, given a huge government which with the best will in the world is infernally hard to budge from bureaucratically-negotiated courses of action, and given at the same time large numbers of Americans who can less and less be whipped into blind support of dubious policies.

Getting from Here to There

How are we to effect changes both in attitude and in policy—changes that are neither trivial or cosmetic? One hopeful sign is that so many Americans in responsible positions believe in their hearts some of these things, or in any event are ready and willing to adopt a new strategy if it seems to make sense. But against that is the weight of the past and the inertia of institutions. Someone once said, "If you take a drunk and put him in a cold shower and feed him black coffee and slap his cheeks and then take him out and dress him—what do you have?" And the answer is: "A wide-awake drunk." Finally, there is the observed fact that people who sound tough are more likely to be admitted to top decision-making circles than those who sound soft.

A cynic once remarked that one of the great things about experience is that it enables you to recognize the same mistake every time you make it. In practice those who run large organizations usually meet any heretical or unorthodox position, not with open arms, but with what might be called a "damage-limiting" strategy. If another built-in obstacle to change is sought, it can be found in the fact that the conduct of U.S. foreign policy has been confined generally to white, middle-aged males, which corresponds neither to the population pattern nor to the diversity of priorities, interests, and viewpoints that pattern reflects.

The people who run governments (at least our own) are neither malevolent nor stupid, despite a disturbingly widespread opinion to the contrary. They are both bright and devoted to the national well-being as they see it. I believe that the Nixon Administration has made some substantial gains in foreign affairs. But the added ingredient that is needed is to overcome what Mr. Nixon likes to call our failure of nerve. I am afraid he was usually thinking of nerve in the sense of acting unilaterally, if necessary, in defense of what is construed as the national interest. For me the needed recovery of nerve is for the purpose of imagining bold and creative designs for a more unified and co-operating world, and having the courage to push them toward reality. It remains true that without vision the people will perish. But with only vision and no follow-through, idealism becomes hypocrisy.

Let me suggest a final litmus-paper test for policy. After we ask, "Is it strategically important?"—which we must, and after we ask, "Is it politically feasible or viable?"—which we must, and after we ask, "Is it cost-effective?"—which we should, perhaps the greatest lesson of Vietnam for the United States is that we should also ask, "Is it humane?" This is not a substitute for the other questions. But only with this additional question can we cure the sickness that has crept into the veins of American foreign policy. The war in Vietnam needed to be ended for us chiefly because it was inhumane; not because we should condone the takeover attempt by the Communist Party of Vietnam, elected by no one; but because other people simply are not going to be saved by being decimated, uprooted and stripped of their culture, whether by us or by any other power.

We can now resolve the paradox of U.S. policy toward Israel. The reason that country's independence represents an important national interest under five Presidents is not based on strategic or economic calculation. In fact, on the basis of such calculation, all other things being equal, we would be better off without it. At least we would say, "Let Israel fend for itself." The reason that Israel seems to represent an important national interest is that millions of Americans, regardless of religion, see it as a *moral* commitment. There seems to be a general sense that those three million people in their democratic society have the right to live and not be exterminated again. This contravenes our oil policy, our wish to limit Soviet influence in the Persian Gulf, and our desire to be friends with the Arabs. But such sense of humanity is the only explanation for policy—or far more an explanation than the votes, which are, after all, fewer than those of some ignored minorities (and even majorities) in America.

Former State Department official Thomas Hughes wrote in *Foreign Affairs* in July 1969:

> Lincoln, Wilson, and [F. D.] Roosevelt at moments of supreme national crisis made our national interest interesting to others by identifying us with ideas that move mankind. And they were not just applying cosmetics to power. They were credible, because they thought the way they talked. Language was close to life, propaganda to performance, public relations to personal commitment.

What an innovation that would be today! And how right. American leaders who still live by fear and mistrust of the American people, by habitual deceit, and by evasion of the clear spirit of the Constitution, deserve the same appeal from the disillusioned American of the center as we should make to our fellow citizens, particularly among the young who have turned in disgust on democracy itself. To both the leadership and the alienated, those of us who have kept the faith but find rot in the church must cry, with Cromwell, "I beseech you, in the bowels of Christ, to think it possible you may be mistaken."

Much of what I have been suggesting in this essay represents continuity with the past, and calls only for rededication to "the unfulfilled potential of this nation," in the incandescent words of the report of the White House Youth Conference. Other actions proposed are novelties, however, and gamble on change. It won't be easy for me and my generation to adopt new attitudes and look at the external world through newly polished lenses. Some of what is required would normally take decades to bring about. Indeed, as the great physicist Max Planck once wrote of comparable difficulties in changing scientific attitudes,

> A new scientific truth does not triumph by convincing its opponents and making them see the light, but rather because its opponents eventually die, and a new generation grows up that is familiar with it. (Cited by T. Kuhn in *The Structure of Scientific Revolutions* [Chicago: University of Chicago Press, 1970], p. 151)

But we don't have generations or even decades if we hope to have this Republic stand proud once again by relating itself to its world in praiseworthy ways. We have to act as though decades and generations had already passed, as if the slow wisdom of time had already come to us; as though (to revise Goethe) the owl of Minerva were to take flight *before* evening falls. Engineers have to "design around" obstacles. A reformed foreign policy has to "design around" both the intransigeance of others and the encrustations in our own arteries.

A story is told of a French general in World War II who visited a detachment in a particularly inhospitable piece of North African desert. He ordered the captain to have a shelter of trees planted. "But, mon Général," protested the captain, "it will take twenty-five years for them to grow." "Indeed?" replied the General. "Then you have no time to lose!"

I have tried to argue that with a change in attitude, policies can still be realistic, national defense can be adequate, and supportable American interests abroad can be protected. With that change, perhaps once again we shall be able to say of this Republic, as that old revolutionary Sam Adams said in April 1775, "What a glorious morning for America!"

INDEX

Anti-Ballistic Missile (ABM), 84, 145
Abu Musa, 162
Acheson, Dean G., 27, 52, 95, 152
Adams, Henry, 130
Adams, John, 62
Adams, Sam, 173
Adorno, T. W., 34
Africa, 81, 156; central, 150; sub-Saharan, 68, 140
Agnew, Spiro, 19, 41, 42, 43, 49
Aid, foreign, 59, 76, 81, 88, 112, 155, 156
Air Force Academy, 20
Airlie House conference 1970, 117
Allende, Salvador, 38
Alliance for Progress, 131
Allison, Graham, 18, 19
Alsop, Joseph, 34
American Bar Association, 103
American Nazi Party, 11
American Security Council, 33
Anderson, Jack, 119
Aqaba, Gulf of, 161
Arab-Israeli Conflict, 67, 77, 85, 139, 158, 161, 162

Archilochus, 45
Arms control, 12, 22, 31, 144, 145, 147, 149, 150
Arms Control and Disarmament Agency, 122, 146
Aron, Raymond, 63
Asia, 29, 59, 82, 87, 154, 156; Southeast, 134, 141

Bach Mai Hospital, 105
Bacon, Francis, 41
Baghdad Pact, 84
Baker, Russell, 125
Balkans, 141
Ball, George, 61
Bay of Pigs, 1961, 93, 96, 104, 105, 168
Beam, Jacob, 69
Becker, Carl, 150
Bentham, Jeremy, 14, 30–31
Berlin, 25, 65, 90, 91, 98
Bermuda Declaration, 8
Bismarck, Otto von, 86, 119, 129, 133
Bohlen, Charles, 69
Bosch, Juan D., 111
Brandt, Willy, 142
Bray, Charles, 115

176 INDEX

Bresler, Robert J., 102
Brezhnev, Leonid, 66
Britain, 28, 59, 67, 85, 118, 121, 141, 143, 151, 152, 160, 167
British Assessments Offices, 121
British General Policy Review Staff, 121
British Liberal Association, 14
Brock, William F., 20
Brodie, Bernard, 92
Bryan, William Jennings, 104
Bulgaria, 161
Bundy, McGeorge, 10, 52, 109, 110, 115, 148
Burke, Admiral Arleigh, 32
Burke, Edmund, 130
Burma, 112

Cambodia, 81, 106, 152, 153, 168
Cambon, Jules, 110
Cambridge Survey Research, 23
Campbell, John Franklin, 55
Camus, Albert, 44, 46
Caribbean, 20, 21, 38
Carnegie Endowment for International Peace, 12, 34
CASCON, 12
Castlereagh, Robert S., 75
Castro, Fidel, 30, 37, 38
Central America, 38
Central Intelligence Agency (CIA), 50, 93, 96, 100
Che Guervarists, 30
Chen Po-ta, 67
Chiang Kai-shek, 102
Chile, 38
China, 25, 31–32, 53, 59, 65, 66, 67, 77, 78, 81, 83, 84, 87, 95, 108, 111, 112, 123, 132, 134, 140, 153, 157, 164, 167

Churchill, Winston, 65, 76, 98, 152
Clausewitz, Karl von, 99
Clay, Henry, 62
Cleveland, Grover, 62
Cold War, 24, 31, 34, 51, 52, 56, 62, 65, 66, 73, 84, 92, 98, 102, 123, 131, 138
Columbia University Bureau of Applied Social Research, 24
Common Market, European, 143
Communications satellites, 159
Congress, U.S., 13, 53, 54, 55, 72, 106, 111, 122, 126, 155, 165
Connally Reservation, 60
Constantinople Convention of 1888, 162
Constitution, U.S., 53, 92, 94, 113, 123, 152, 172
Cooley, John K., 80
Costa Rica, 81
Council on Foreign Relations, 11, 12, 23, 34, 50, 54
Cromwell, Oliver, 172
Cuba, 21, 37, 81, 96, 104, 153 (*see also* Bay of Pigs)
Cuban missile crisis, 1962, 91, 139
Cyprus, 118
Czechoslovakia, 106, 140, 168

Davignon Committee, 143
Davis, Norman H., 101
Defense, Department of, 4, 50, 64, 67, 89, 90, 91, 93, 105, 106, 108, 116, 148
De Gaulle, Charles, 79
Diem, Ngo Dinh, 86
Dillon, Douglas T., 52
Dominican Republic, 37, 105, 111, 134, 168

INDEX

Dulles, John Foster, 23, 52, 63, 70, 75, 81, 84, 85, 86, 102, 103, 104, 152, 153, 160
Durrell, Lawrence, 118

East Germany, 89, 91
East Pakistan, 77, 81, 119, 157, 158, 167
Eden, Anthony, 66, 86
Edwards, Jonathan, 62, 141
Egypt, 85, 160, 161, 167, 168
Eisenhower, Dwight D., 14, 60, 76, 78, 83, 94, 98, 109, 112
Eisenhower Doctrine, 85
Ellsberg, Daniel, 108, 113
Emerson, Ralph Waldo, 62
Engels, Friedrich, 46
Establishment, 13, 17, 19, 20, 21, 49, 50, 54, 55, 61, 73, 83, 123, 144
Ethiopia, 81
Europe, 5, 29, 39, 53, 59, 65, 75, 91, 92, 94, 98, 120, 141, 142, 156; Central, 95; Conference on Security and Cooperation, 119, 140, 143; Eastern, 56, 64, 68, 76, 89, 90, 140, 156; Reduction of military forces, 119; Western, 57, 58, 65, 119, 120, 143, 144, 162
Executive agreements, 111

Fallaci, Oriana, 152
Federal Bureau of Investigation (FBI), 42
Flexible Response, 131
Ford Foundation, 34
Foreign Service, U.S., 55, 115, 117
France, 38, 85, 102, 117, 143, 152, 160, 167
Frankel, Max, 87
Freedom House, 61

Friedheim, Jerry, 105
Fulbright, J. William, 108
Galtung, Johan, 39
Gallup Poll, 16, 26, 100
Gaming, political, 4, 5, 97, 116
Gavin, General, 97
Gearin, Cornelius J., 97
General Accounting Office, 122
Geneva Agreement of 1954, 78, 105, 107
Georgetown University, 32
Germany, 8, 37, 40, 67
German Peace Treaty, 91, 94
Gerson, Louis L., 102
Ghana, 167
Goa, 167
Goldwater, Barry, 49, 102, 123
Greece, 76, 77, 80, 153, 154
Griffith, William E., 11
Guatemala, 88

Hagen, Everett, 11
Haiphong, 107, 112
Harriman, Averell, 52
Harris, Patricia, 113
Harvard University, 4, 18, 23, 40, 44, 55, 94
Heath, Edward, 121
Herter, Christian, 116
Herter Committee Report, 63
Hiss, Alger, 11
Hitler, Adolf, 66, 81 (see also Nazism)
Ho Chi Minh, 78
Hobbes, Thomas, 45
Hoffer, Eric, 39
Honolulu Conference, 109
Hook, Sidney, 45
Hoopes, Townsend, 53, 56
Hoover, Herbert, 156
Hormuz, Strait of, 162
House of Representatives, 123
House Un-American Activities Committee, 40

Houston, Tom Charles, 42
Hughes, Thomas, 172
Hull, Cordell, 101
Hungary, 85, 89, 102, 140, 161, 168
Hurok, Sol, 68
Hyderabad, 167

ICBM, 146
India, 151, 152, 157, 167
India-Pakistan Conflict, 81, 119, 139, 154, 156, 158
Indian Ocean, 68, 140–41
Indochina, French, 152 (*see also* Vietnam)
Indonesia, 162, 167
International Court of Justice, 60, 160, 166
International Peace Academy, 12
International Petroleum Company, 38
International Studies Association, 117
Iran, 81 (*see also* Persia)
Irwin, John, 38
Israel, 25, 36, 77, 85, 134, 151, 160, 167, 171
Italy, 25
International Telephone and Telegraph Corp. (ITT), 38

Jackson, Henry M., 33
Jackson, Stonewall, 109
Japan, 37, 57, 65, 112, 140, 156, 162
Janis, Irving, 93
Jefferson, Thomas, 40, 76
John Birch Society, 11, 54
Johnson, Louis, 90
Johnson, Lyndon B., 8, 14, 37, 60, 76, 83, 94, 100, 102, 105, 107, 123
Joint War Games Agency, 116

Kellen, Konrad, 71
Kennan, George, 69, 70, 82
Kennedy, John F., 14, 26, 63, 76, 80, 96, 104, 105, 115, 123, 139
Keynes, Maynard, 37
Khan, Yahya, 157
Kintner, William, 34
Kissinger, Henry A., 10, 70, 75, 76, 77, 94, 114, 115, 119, 122, 153, 154, 158
Klingberg, Frank L., 27
Kohler, Foy, 69
Kolko, Gabriel, 51, 52, 53, 54
Korea, 8, 84, 90, 92, 93, 95, 96, 109, 153
Khrushchev, Nikita S., 45, 65, 67, 91, 105
Kuhn, Thomas, 171

Laird, Melvin, 3, 4, 94, 105
Lake, Anthony, 107, 112
Laloy, Jean, 57
Laos, 81, 100, 105, 108, 134, 153
Latin America, 36, 38, 43, 68, 81, 104, 150
Lausanne, Treaty of, 1923, 161
Lavelle, John D., 107
League of Nations, 101
Lebanon, 1958, 108
Left (wing), 9, 18, 24, 28, 29, 30, 35, 36, 37, 38, 39, 40, 41, 45, 50, 54, 68, 73, 82, 89, 136
Leiss, Amelia, 25
Lend-Lease, 65, 156
Lenin, V. I., 31, 36, 37
Liberia, 81
Liberty Lobby, 34
Lincoln, Abraham, 27, 28, 62, 76, 110, 126, 169, 172
Lindsay, John, 26
Lin Piao, 65

INDEX

Lippmann, Walter, 27
Lodge, Henry Cabot, 52
Long, Huey, 110
Lovett, Robert, 52
Lowell, Robert, 68
Luxemburg, Rosa, 30, 37

MacArthur, Douglas, 109
Malacca, Strait of, 162
Malaysia, 162, 167
Malenkov, Georgi M., 67
Mailer, Norman, 39
Mao Tse-tung, 33, 81, 87, 89, 112
Marcuse, Herbert, 39
Marshall Plan, 156
Marxism, 33, 40, 46, 50, 65, 67, 69, 82, 87, 150
McCarthy, Joseph R., 103, 110
McCloy, John J., 52
McCone, John, 52
McNamara, Robert, 83, 94, 99, 148
Mediterranean, 68, 80, 86, 140
Meo Tribesmen, 100
Metternich, Prince C. W. L., 75
Middle East, 22, 36, 53, 65, 77, 85, 86, 108, 154, 158 (see also Arab-Israeli Conflict)
Millikan, Max F., 116
Mill, John Stuart, 14
MIRV, 84, 149
Massachusetts Institute of Technology (M.I.T.), 4, 6, 7, 8, 9, 18, 25, 37, 86, 94, 116, 156
Molotov, Vvasheslav M., 67
Montreux Convention, 162
Moorer, Admiral Thomas H., 94
Morgenthau, Hans J., 82
Moscow summit, 1972, 66
Munich Agreement, 1938, 66, 135, 137
Murphy, Robert, 103

Napoleon Bonaparte, 134
Nasser, Gamal Abdel, 66, 102, 167
National Security Council (NSC), 4, 33, 60, 68, 84, 90, 92, 97, 98, 115
National War College, 11
NATO, 81, 84, 91, 95, 120, 142
Naval Academy, U.S., 20
Nazism, 58, 70 (see also Hitler, Adolf)
Neustadt, Richard, 113
New Deal, 53
Newsweek, 17
New York Herald Tribune, 101
New York Liberal Party, 14
New York Times, 8, 16, 17, 19, 21, 39, 87
Nicolson, Harold, 110
Nitze, Paul, 90
Nixon, Richard M., 5, 11, 14, 21, 22, 24, 26, 31, 32, 34, 42, 43, 49, 50, 59, 63, 67, 70, 75, 76, 77, 87, 94, 100, 106, 123, 124, 125, 139, 153, 154, 157, 163, 170
Nixon Doctrine, 153, 155, 169
North Africa, 140
Nuclear Non-Proliferation Treaty, 147
Nuclear weapons, 90, 144, 145, 147, 148, 149

Oil, 37, 162
Olney, Richard, 62
Organization of American States, 81
Ostpolitik, 142
Ostrower, Gary B., 101
Outer space, 160
Oxford Union, 21

Pacific Ocean, 59
Pakistan, 77, 154, 157

INDEX

Pakistan, East, see East Pakistan
Palestine, 39, 85, 151, 158
Panama Canal, 160, 161
Paris Commune, 46
Paris summit conference, 109
Pearl Harbor, 71, 131
P'eng Teh-huai, 67
Pentagon Papers, 27, 105, 108, 110
Perkins, Milo, 23
Persia, 141 (see also Iran)
Persian Gulf, 68, 162, 171
Peru, 38
Philippines, 81
Planck, Max, 172
Poland, 89, 140
Policy planning, 60, 85, 86, 90, 96, 114, 115, 116, 119, 120, 121, 122
Portugal, 81
Poseidon missile, 148
Potomac Associates, 26
Potsdam Conference, 1945, 162
Powers, Francis Gary, 109
Princeton University, 55
Pye, Lucian, 11

Quemoy and Matsu, 102
Quigg, Philip, 54

Rand Corporation, 71, 116
Rapacki, Adam, 95
Red Army, 64
Reedy, George, 121, 124
regional organizations, 167 (see also by name)
Reich, Charles, 44, 113
Reston, James, 110
Revisionist history, 51, 52, 55, 61
Rhodesia, 163
Richardson, Elliot L., 3, 113, 116
Richardson, Warren, 34

Right (wing), 28, 29, 32, 41, 42, 45, 164
Rockefeller Foundation, 34
Rockefeller, John D. III, 21, 22
Rogers, William P., 3
Romney, George, 133
Rooney, John J., 116
Roosevelt, Franklin D., 14, 98, 101, 115, 152, 172
Roosevelt, Theodore, 62
Rostow, Walt W., 10, 83, 115, 116
Rousseau, Jean Jacques, 40
Romania, 89, 161
Rusk, Dean, 3, 52, 66
Russell, Bertrand, 57

Saar, 66
Salinger, Pierre, 109
SALT agreement, 24, 33, 53, 66, 84, 109, 139, 146, 147
Samuelson, Paul, 37
Sartre, Jean-Paul, 39
Schelling, Thomas C., 32, 122
Schweitzer, Albert, 130
Seabed, 160
SEATO, 84
Senate, U.S., 19, 123; Foreign Relations Committee, 53, 99; Select Committee on Watergate, 23
Shannon, William, 39
Shulman, Marshall, 70
Sihanouk, Prince Norodom, 152
Singapore, 162
Sino-Soviet dispute, 30, 33, 84
Sontay raid, 106, 108
Southern Africa, 36, 60
Soviet Union, 11, 12, 13, 17, 21, 24, 25, 28, 29, 30, 31, 32, 33, 34, 35, 40, 43, 45, 46, 51, 56, 57, 58, 59, 60, 61, 63, 64, 65, 66, 67, 68, 69, 70, 71, 72, 73, 74, 75, 76,

INDEX

77, 78, 79, 81, 82, 83, 84, 86, 87, 89, 90, 92, 94, 95, 98, 99, 102, 106, 108, 109, 111, 131, 132, 134, 135, 138, 139, 140, 141, 142, 143, 144, 145, 148, 149, 150, 151, 153, 156, 157, 161, 162, 163, 166, 167, 168, 171; Institute of the U.S.A., 12, 70
Spain, 76, 80, 81, 105
Stalin, Joseph, 56, 65, 69, 72, 81, 90, 99
State, Department of, 4, 6, 11, 12, 23, 30, 53, 62, 68, 85, 87, 90, 93, 97, 101, 112, 114, 115, 116, 117, 118, 119, 120, 121, 122, 172
Stevenson, Adlai E., 104
Stilwell, Joseph W., 112
Stormer, John A., 11
Strachan, Gordon, 23
Straits, international, 160, 161, 162, 167
Strangelove, Dr., 88
Strausz-Hupé, Robert, 34
Students for Democratic Society (SDS), 9, 11
Sudetenland, 66
Suez Canal, 85, 102, 160, 161, 162
Sulzberger, C. L., 49, 63, 86
Summit meetings, 141
Surplus Marketing Administration, U.S., 23

Taft, William Howard, 37
Taiwan, 81, 111, 153, 164
Talmon, J. L., 39
Taylor, Maxwell, 83
Test-ban treaty, 1963, 150
Thailand, 25, 82, 153
Thieu, Nguyen van, 77, 86

Third World, 12, 22, 37, 50, 51, 54, 58, 66, 67, 88, 92, 98, 150, 152, 154
Thucydides, 152
Thurber, James, 41
Thompson, Llewellyn, 69
Tibet, 167
Time, 25
Tiran, Strait of, 161, 167
Titoism, 33, 58
Tonkin Gulf Resolution, 89
Trendex, 24
Trotsky, Leon, 132
Truman, Harry, 14, 94, 112, 162
Tunb (islands), 162
Tupamaros, 39
Turkey, 76, 81, 153-54
Turkish Straits, 161

U-2 flights, 60, 109
Underground nuclear tests, 150
United Nations, 11, 12, 13, 19, 30, 34, 59, 60, 81, 85, 86, 90, 98, 104, 111, 112, 113, 162, 163, 164, 165, 166, 167; Charter, 64, 83, 103, 167, 168; Conference on the Environment, 159; Day, 11; General Assembly, 103, 166-67; Genocide Convention, 60; observer group, 168; peacekeeping, 162, 168; Presidential Commission on Future of, 164; sanctions, 163; Security Council, 33, 81, 103, 166; Special Emergency General Assembly, 85

Vandenberg, Arthur H., Jr., 14
Vienna Summit, 105
Vietcong, 9, 38
Vietminh, 78

Vietnam, North, 65, 81, 84, 105, 106, 107, 108, 112, 134, 168
Vietnam, South, 8, 32, 36, 77, 78, 81, 86, 87, 100, 105, 106, 107, 134, 154
Vietnam War, 6, 7, 8, 9, 14, 17, 18, 19, 22, 23, 25, 26, 28, 32, 35, 36, 38, 43, 53, 54, 56, 57, 66, 82, 83, 85, 89, 93, 94, 95, 96, 97, 100, 102, 105, 106, 107, 108, 109, 110, 113, 121, 123, 135, 142, 152, 153, 154, 157, 162, 171

Wald, George, 68
Walker, Lannon, 115
Wallace, George, 110
Wall Street Journal, 24, 25
Washington, George, 62
Watergate, 16, 26, 27, 100, 108, 123, 124
Weathermen, 8, 9, 39
Westmoreland, William C., 83
West Point, 20
Wheeler, Earle, 3
White House Conference on Youth, 19, 20, 172
Williams, G. Mennen, 116
Wilson, Woodrow, 63, 83, 129, 134, 153, 172
Wolfe, Bertram, 74
Wooten, Sir Henry, 101
World War II, 56, 64, 84, 156
Washington Special Action Group (WSAG), 119

Yale University, 55
Yalta Agreement, 118
Yarmolinsky, Adam, 94
Yemen, 167
York, Herbert, 99
Yost, Charles W., 98
Young Turks, 114, 116

Ziegler, Ronald, 108, 158, 159
Zumwalt, Elmo, 113